Five Irrefutable Problems with Christianity

By Darayah Yahuwdah Bin Yishrayil

DORRANCE PUBLISHING CO
EST. 1920
PITTSBURGH, PENNSYLVANIA 15238

Dorrance Publishing Co
585 Alpha Drive
Suite 103
Pittsburgh, PA 15238
Visit our website at www.dorrancebookstore.com

ISBN: 979-8-8868-3193-1
eISBN: 979-8-8868-3766-7

Introduction

I'm going to begin the introduction of this study by qualifying myself with a much abbreviated biographical summation of spiritual and religious background, just so as not to be misconstrued as novas to scriptural studies. While this does not include extensive elaboration of my experiences in the street life, drug abuse, or the shadier side. I only mention it here briefly just to say that, I'm just an average Joe Shmo, seeking no special recognition of any great accomplishments, or exaltation over anybody else. When I was a boy, with rare exception, I did all the things boys typically do. When I was a young man I didn't do anything exceptional or especially out of the ordinary, and due to a great deal of faulty decisions on my part, the conclusion of my youth was a time which marks and encapsulates the very worst days of my life. Though my parents did everything necessary to prevent it, I took it upon myself to learn the ways of the street; the only benefit of which is the learning experience that, while not being recommended, must still not be denied. It was a stage of my life that I am grateful to have survived, and to have outgrown. You'll have to read "The Basic Text" of recovery if further details of such is where your interests lay. The point here is as I repeat, I'm not looking for any kind of exaltation over others. I'm not holy, especially good, I'm not an angel, I'm not perfect, or "Reverend", as some like to be called. I'm just a regular guy; a human being; in flesh; subject to all, and guilty of many of the faults common to Man. So why should you listen to me? Don't. However, despite my faults, a few years ago I stumbled across some information that I now dare publicly share:

Present subject matter begins on Thor's Day; the second day of the second month of the Gregorian year nineteen sixty-one, when I was first to emerge through the matrix into this plane of existence through the portal of a so-called "African American" whose name was Sarah, and by means of Christian family members, I was taken to various churches throughout my childhood. Because of the hypocrisy perceived to have stemmed from both the leadership and the attendant congregation of the churches they had visited in their formative years, the overwhelming majority of the men of my family, including my father, Donald, like most so-called Christians, rarely if ever went into any of those various places of worship after coming of age, therefore it was primarily the women of my family that frequented those establishments, and led by them, I was introduced to several denominations of this particular branch of Abrahamic religions, more specifically known as the Apostolic, Baptist, Catholic, Methodist, etc.

Like many, they started me off going to Sunday School as a tiny tot, when I was about twelve however, having been overcome by years of mounting curiosity regarding the behaviors I had observed in these churches, the Apostolic most particularly, since that was the one my mother regularly attended at that time. I desired to know how those behaviors corresponded with the words written in the book by which the people claimed to be so inspired, and thus I began to read. As the years continued to pass, I secretly read The King James Version of The Bible from cover to cover, Genesis to Revelation; by the time I was twenty three, I had done so three times, and it was at about that time, transformed and inspired by the birth of my eldest daughter, and by my growing desire to be the best man that I could, I became a very devout Christian, and was baptized into the Seventh-day Adventist Church, where I remained and served as a deacon and Sabbath-school teacher for about fourteen years.

During that time, one of the first consistencies I couldn't help but notice is that most self-identified Christians rarely if ever attend church at all; going there only on special occasions like funerals, weddings, and certain holidays. More significant is the rarity at which they read the Bible; thereby leaving themselves willfully ignorant, and vulnerably led, misled, and deceived by those in leadership positions who are often equally as "in the dark", ignorant as the fools who follow them. Since I also noticed the great difficulty with which most people struggle to decipher the code of these writings, their clarification quickly became a motivating factor for me. That is to say; I desired both then and now, to do my very best to clarify scripture, and make it easier for the average person to comprehend. With such knowledge and understanding, I hope that they would lead themselves out of the darkness, and bondage of the ignorance in which I've never found any personal bliss, contrarily finding it much more so in the light of knowledge instead. Thankfully, I do believe that I've been fortunate enough to have assisted several people in this endeavor, and with that I have learned to make myself content to share with babes requiring milk, children requiring bread moistened thereby, meat for the rarely encountered adults able to digest it, and no longer seeking martyrdom, I keep my peace when wisdom deems it necessary, because as I've also noticed, after having obtained a desired level of knowledge, most people settle into an acquired comfort-zone, which may be even less penetrable than that of those less knowledgeably fortunate. In other words, "they", after gaining a certain level of knowledge, desire "no mas"; they desire to go no further, and will fight in order to maintain the perfect bliss and stability of the walls bordering the fortress of those comfort-zones.

This has never been my way; even now my thirst remains unquenched, and my hunger insatiable. The cumulative effect being: The older I get, the more I learn. Yes the more I learn, the more I know, but the more I know, the more I know I don't know. We humans are actually quite limited by the bounds of our five or six senses. Thus constantly compelled to add, and adding here that, during my studies I have also acquired some knowledge of Hinduism, the significance of Deep Breathing (Gen.2:7),Transcendental Meditation, and Islam as well; having previously associated myself with several Moslem, and Muslim acquaintances, and occasionally attending various halls, mosques, and temples along the way. I've also read once through the Bhagavad-Gita. However, because I find the "Blood Oath Covenant", made between Yahuwah and the children of Yishrayil, encompassed within those six degrees of law known as Shamath, Shemoth, Exodus, nineteen through twenty-four, to be much more personally, and fundamentally compelling, and though I have seen great light in their literature, customs, and philosophy, I have chosen not to sustain religious orthodoxy among neither Buddhists, Hindus nor Islamic faiths.

Around the age of thirty-seven (1998), my studies having continually progressed, then led me to question Christianity, and though I diligently searched among the pastors, deacons, and respected members of the congregation, finding no satisfactory answers to those questions, in nineteen ninety-nine, undaunted by any of the typical **scare tactics** they employ, such as the anathema of being labeled apostate, blasphemer, heretic, and being threatened with brimstone, hell fire, etc", I departed that church and went even deeper into my own studies. Having completed hundreds of considerations by the time the outline for the following report was formulated in two thousand nine, many of the discrepancies of Christianity having long sense been revealed to me; I had therefore ceased identifying myself as a Christian, nor claimed I membership of any other "Religion". I did however for quite a while identify myself as a Messianic Hebrew Yishrayiliy. At that stage of my journey, I initially thought that this man, Yahawashi, Yahuwshua, Yahshua, Isa, etc., as the Quraan, and its Muslim adherents teach, had actually been a historically factual prophet. Secondly, I thought that since I no longer "worshiped" him; a practice strictly forbidden by The Torah, in which repetitive and emphatic commands are given us, to worship and serve no one and nothing other than Yah and Yah alone. This being a principle frequently contrasted by the writers of the "New Testament"; Matt 28:9, Mark 5:6, Luke 24:52, John 9:38 as but a few of many citable examples, and thirdly, after acquisition of sufficient information, I no longer called him Jesus, as if that actually mattered. Truth is, no matter what name is used, the narrative of the story remains consistent. For such reasons, I thought I was somehow better off, and wiser than those who continue to do so. I didn't consider Messianic Hebraism to be a religion, but a life-style, a culture, and more significantly, a genealogy of people of which I had descended. These concepts being based on the spiritual principles revealed in a strict adherence to the teachings of Torah, and Tanakh, which many Christians actually belittle by calling it, "The Old Testament"; viewing it as presently invalid, due to the assumed fact that they have a "New Testament" that, as they say, "does away with" "The Old" by "hanging it upon The Cross".

Yet while conducting research on the prophesied Kingdom of Yah (Ps.68:4), and the throne of Malik Dawiyd, more readily known as King David, I inadvertently stumbled across some information in which I initially found great discomfort. If what I had found proved to be true, it would shatter the **belief system** upon which I had based my entire life. It troubled me so, because I knew that once again it was time for me to learn, and that learning had so often proven to be such a painful process. It was time for me to grow, but worst of all, once again, it was time for me to change. While change is indeed the most persistent universal principle, it is often found that among those of us who are in similitude to the principle of physics, where in objects deemed stationary tend to remain as such, and moving objects tend to remain in motion; in empathy with the reader, with age, and/or a satisfactory level of life experience, we too tend to become inflexibly set in our own ways of thinking and behaving. Understating its uncomfortability, we all agree that change, even for the better, can prove to be very difficult to say the least.

Now while it's not my desire to disturb anyone's peace; in fact I initially thought merely to share my concerns with my close friends, and scripture study partners, sincerely hoping that their research might somehow disprove my own. However today, after having done so, and after our very careful consideration, I now know that the facts, and principles I'm about to share with you are true beyond the shadow of all doubt. This is a statement in which I do not mean to insinuate having found all the answers; no one save "The Creator of All" may accurately make such a lofty claim. In fact this study, while answering many questions, also raises many others, but if you choose to push forward, as I hope you do, I feel that it is only fair of me to warn you that you are about to see just as I did; that we had previously fallen victim to great deception. I must also inform you that in the day that you accept the contents of this little pamphlet, by then you too will have experienced the same type of spiritual and emotional wrestling elaborated of Yaaqob Bin Yitzkhaq, at the conclusion of which, as recorded in Barashiyth: the thirty-second degree; verses twenty-four to thirty-two, he walked with a limp, and his name was changed from Yaaqob, a dishonorable name that means thief or usurper; to the honorable name of Yishrayil, which means; Man that rules with The Strong One, or Man who rules with strength. Yet another definition of this name has been rendered, Man who rules as Yah would rule. The encoded allegory is of one wrestling with self as they suffer the process of withdrawal from previously held misbeliefs that confine us to ignorance and idolatry. The end of which leaves a spiritual vacuum that must be filled by the acquisition, of right knowledge, right wisdom, and right understanding. You will have joined the one percent who have opted to reject "The Blue Pill". Your mind will have been freed, and the remainder of you will certainly follow.

Most of those with whom I've had the honor and privilege of sharing this information, have not only rejected it, but have apparently afterwards fallen off the face of this flat earth, and are subsequently never seen nor heard from again; I say this sarcastically as **I am not a "Flat Earther"**, but I say this in reference to the disappearance of those introduced earlier as, "my close friends, and Scripture Study partners". However I still nevertheless encourage the most courageous of readers to either confirm, or at least attempt to deny my research with your own. Your challenge, as of now, regarding this book, is to take whatever time is necessary to read every word, to literally open your Bible, and read every scriptural reference given herein, and citing others of your choosing, get back to me with your results as soon as possible. At which time I hope to be granted a chance at rebuttal, in order to prove that, each, and every reference in the Law, Prophets, and the writings thereof; the so-called, "Old Testament", to which one might be tempted to appoint as prophetic mention of a coming Messiah, can very easily be shown to have absolutely nothing to do with one named Jesus Christ. I thank you in anticipation of your cooperation, and will always gladly welcome your intelligent input.

Five Irrefutable Problems with Christianity

The five most significant problems with the branch of Abrahamic religion known as Christianity are here alphabetically listed, and also serve as the respective titles for the short chapters of this pamphlet:

Cannibalism
Human Sacrifice
Idolatry
Messy Genealogy
Paganism

At the onset, I'd like to clarify the fact that, while this work is obviously open to public dissemination, the target audience is the descendants of the enslaved; survivors of the Transatlantic Slave Trade, as well as the remnant of those of us that were already here in the far west hundreds of years previous to being "discovered" by Columbus, and the massive European invasion and subsequent emigration to the Americas. This due, not only to that which we've all been taught in History class, but also my own experiential observations of the position and condition in-which we currently find ourselves. By means of the clarification of Hebrew Scripture, I've been given the answers to many of the fundamental questions we've all been asking, and only hope to share my findings.

After having shattered their state of denial, most Christians feel shocked, surprised, and like a duped virgin, betrayed when they learn of the relative gravity of the truth that all of the above, "forbidden practices", are fundamentally interwoven into the very fabric of their coerced, and/or otherwise chosen religion, as the compilation of scriptural references in this pamphlet will prove to anyone ready, willing, and able to read them.

Yahuwah is Our Mighty-One, and it is Yah to whom we must return. More clearly stated; the overwhelming majority; even as much as 97% of the Europeans, most popularly known as Jews, are of Ashkenazi, Khazarian,Yiddish descent, and as such are neither Shamitic nor Hebraic in their genetic lineage (Gen.10:1-5), and those that are Shamitic, as few as 3%, are Edomites (It is misnomer and false doctrine to believe and teach that all Europeans, so-called "White people", Gentiles are Edomites, when scripture study [Gen.36:1-16] reveals that Edom's first two wives were Kanaaniym, Canaanites; Adah who was a Khittiy, Hittite, and her cousin named Aholiybamah who was a Khiwwiy, Hivite; these are Germanic, "White People", Gentiles, which makes obvious the fact that "White People" existed long before Esau, Edom was even born), and therefore cannot possibly fit the very specific biblical description of a woolly haired (Dan.7:9), dark-skinned (Gen.2:25, Dan.7:9, Rev.1:15), lost, and destitute people, still suffering the self-imposed ravages of "Blood Oath Violation". The children of Yishrayil broke a covenant, which is also known as an "Unbreakable Vow" (Ex.19-24, Lev.26, Deut.28), and even now as I write, and you read, continue to experience, with the exception of that withheld by Yah's mercy, the consequential horrors expected to result there from. The impostors (Rev.2:9, 3:9) who had more than just a glimpse, but had full knowledge of this truth, had no intention of revealing it for public dissemination. Due to both the willful ignorance of the masses, and the "crafty counsel" of Media Moguls, predominated by powerful members of the previously mentioned family of impostors, stumbling blocks are cast before the blind, and this secret remains among the world's best kept. It is Yahawah's will however, that such truths will not remain hidden, and is even now in the process of being revealed to an awakening world (Eze.37:1-14).

1. Cannibalism

The very first commandment recorded in the Hebrew Scripture is "Be fruitful and multiply" (Gen.1:22 & 28), which is obviously contrary to Cannibalism, and Human Sacrifice. Homosexuality might also be considered here, but because it is a subject, covertly practiced, but not overtly sanctioned by The Church, I won't include elaboration on that particular subject in this pamphlet. Both Cannibalism, and Human Sacrifice result in a form of subtraction and/or culling of population, which in itself is obviously contrary to the principles of population growth, or "fruitful multiplication". Yet both these despicable acts were in deed practiced by the children of Yishrayil, the one actually producing the other. That is; Human Sacrifice was forbidden by Yah. It was but one of the appalling acts perfected by the nations that had previously provoked Him to anger, and for which cause He had destroyed them. When Yishrayil began to practice these same acts, it naturally brought about the same basic results. Along with the added betrayal Yah felt, as it was He who had personally groomed them. Yah had walked them through the process of nation building, starting with one man and wife, Abraham and Sharah, to a family group, clans, tribes, and eventually, they were set up in their own land as a sovereign nation. Yah was sorely disappointed when Yishrayil needlessly, and voluntarily turned their backs on Him, in order to work and ship for; "work-ship"; worship "hinder gods"; this term; "hinder gods", is speaking of those previously worshiped, or those that had been left behind. This intern provoked Yah to anger, and He subsequently allowed their enemies to besiege them to the point of starvation; at which desperate point, instead of repenting, they resorted to taking matters in their own hands, and some of them were found guilty of consuming one another; they even ate their own children. Is it really so hard to believe? Here confirm a couple scriptural verses of the same:

Yishayah/Isaiah 9:19-21

The land was dark with the wrath of Yahuwah's armies: the people were taking men's flesh for food. On the right a man was cutting off bits and was still in need; on the left a man took a meal but had not enough; no man had pity on his brother; everyone was making a meal of the flesh of his neighbor. Manasseh was making a meal of Ephraim, and Ephraim of Manasseh; and together they were attacking Yahuwdah. For all this Yah's wrath is not turned away, but his hand is stretched out still.

While reading the writings accredited to the prophet Yahazaqal, Yechetzqyah, Ezekiel, I was astounded by the accuracy with which he so precisely described what was simultaneously going on in the U S A. Thus I want to strongly encourage Yishrayil to read his words and share in my amazement (Eze.5:1-17). The following excerpt is verse 5-13:

This is what Yahuwah said: This is Yarushaluwm: I have put her among the nations, and countries surround her on every side. She has disobeyed my orders by <u>doing more evil than the other nations</u>, and against my rules more than the countries around her: for they have given up my orders, and as for my rules, they have not gone in the way of them. For this cause I, Yahuwah have said: Because you have been more uncontrolled than the nations round about you, and have not been guided by my rules or kept my orders, but have kept the orders of the nations round about you; For this cause **Yahuwah has said: Even I am against you**; and I will be judging among you before the eyes of the nations. I will do in you what I have not done and will not do again, because of all your disgusting ways. For this cause fathers will (literally) take their sons for food among you, and sons will (literally) make a meal of their fathers; and I will be judge among you, and all the rest of you I will send away to every wind. For this cause, by my life, says Yahuwah (This is Yah swearing by his own existence and mortality, which proves that, all the Elohiym, though long lived, many thousands of years beyond our life spans, are indeed mortal), because you have made my holy place unclean with all your hated things and all your disgusting ways, you have become disgusting to me; my eye will have no mercy and I will have no pity. A third of you will come to death from disease, wasting away among you through need of food; a third will be put to the sword round about you; and a third I will send away to every wind, *letting loose a sword after you*. So my wrath will be complete and my passion will come to rest on you; and they will be certain that <u>I, Yahuwah have given the word of decision</u>, when my wrath against them is complete.

It is truly incredible when we consider the scriptural fact that, Yah's plan was that we should be the earth's number one nation. It was Yah's plan that we would in all ways be situated as the head of all nations and never as the tail. We often find ourselves wondering why, not only does the so-called, "White Man" hate us, but every nation and people of the earth; whether Black, Brown, Red, Yellow, or White, they either hate or simply feel indifferent toward us. I've often heard the scripturally ignorant,   whether Yishrayilite or gentile, while thinking out loud they all express their wonder as to why, and I long to share the following truth with them: Truth is; it wouldn't matter how the other nations felt about us, if we were with Yah, and He with us (imaniul), but there are actually several scriptural references, some of which I will here share, that state the fact that even Yah Himself is rightfully against us. If they would simply read the Hebrew Scripture, the Bible, if they would study the very books that they've been falsely taught to believe have been "done away" and "hung on a cross"; and by which some falsely claim to be so inspired; if they would simply read, even the spiritually blind would see, that even though Yah said He'd gladly accept the blame, He actually can't truly be blamed, as it was we and our ancestors that foolishly and repetitively turned our backs on Him. Since then we are receiving in ourselves the recompense of our error, which is meet. From a Karmic universe, we are getting exactly what our hands called for (Lev.26:40-42).

2 Kings 6:24-30

After this Ben-hadad king of Syria gathered all his army and went up and lay siege to Samaria. In addition there was a great famine in Samaria, and they besieged it until a donkey's head sold for 2 lbs of silver, and a half pint of pigeon shit sold for 2 oz. of silver. As the king of Yishrayil was passing by on the wall, a woman cried to him, saying, Help, my lord, O king! And he said, if

Yahuwah doesn't help you, how can I help you? Out of the barn-floor, or out of the wine press? And the king said to her, "What ails you?" She said, "This woman said to me, "Give your son so that we may eat him today, and we will eat my son tomorrow". So we boiled my son and ate him. And I said to her on the other day, "Give your son so that we may eat him." And now she has hidden her son". When the king heard the words of the woman, he tore his clothes as he passed by on the wall, and everybody noticed that he was wearing sackcloth underwear.

Now the point here, not lost on me is the fact that, the situation being depicted here is during the time after they had already consumed all the cattle, sheep, goats, chicken, horses, swine, and yes I mean the pigs feet, hog mogs, and shitterleans; for there is no part of the pig that you won't eat. They had already consumed all the dogs, cats, rats, mice, squirrels, rabbits, insects, and were down to the last of the donkeys, and pigeons, which were being reserved for the very richest, and highest ranking of the people remaining in the region. The poor had to eat anything they could get their hands on, including one another; the stronger ate the weaker. Can you imagine the horror? People looking and lusting after one another as an entree? Women were consuming their own children? I would call it, "unbelievable", if I hadn't seen our unrelinquished determination, and propensity toward idolatry with my own eyes, having frequently heard, and previous to repentance, even I having spoken the words of modern Yaaqob's protest. All of which clearly illustrates the deeply rooted establishment of this religion. There yet remain too many among us who would rather perfect cannibalism, than to worship Yah and Yah alone.

According to Genesis 3: 12 & 13, and as seen by our own experiences, we humans have a tendency to blame others for our own self-destructive behavior. Dad blamed Mom and Yah, while Mom blamed Nakhash, but truth is that 100 % of all blame is rightfully placed on the individual whose troubles are self-inflicted; each one must be self-held accountable, for only then may an individual, or group hope to recover. This being so, who will we blame now Yishrayil for the predicament in-which we find ourselves? Should we blame the enemy under whom we now find ourselves subservient? Mosheh warned, and prophesied that for our covenant violation, Yahuwah would bring us back into an Egypt like form of slavery, but that this time we'd be transported there by means of slave-ships (No other people more perfectly fit this description): and that we'd be sold to our enemies as bondmen, and bondwomen, and that no one would prevent such a sale, nor in anywise rescue us (Deut.28:68). Every such transaction requires both a buyer, and a seller, but now with the current focus of most of us being so intensely centered upon the buyer, the seller has almost totally been forgotten. In the grip of ignorance and selective amnesia, the fact that Hamitic economies were primary among those that became wealthy reliant upon the capture and sale of our ancestors into this latest, but not first of many captivities, has now been largely disregarded. It may be difficult for some to believe, but the maritime records clearly show, that for two hundred years, ships sailed from West Africa, primarily toward the Americas, carrying a cargo of slaves. During which time, more than two hundred and fifty million souls were lost during the process of capture, storage, and shipping; not to mention the tally of horrors experienced after diasporatic landing. It's a shame to hear of the six million Jews that Hitler slaughtered, but that number pales in comparison to the holocaust that has yet to end among the true Yishrayiliym. Since the German slaughter of Jews didn't result in the establishment of Yah's Kingdom, and the oppressor's yoke remains upon his neck, it is obvious that we yet await the climatic end of Yaaqob's trouble. We must also be considerate of the fact that, most of the merchant shipping companies earlier here mentioned, were owned by the Yiddish impostor.

Again I ask, who should we blame now Yishrayil, for the predicament in-which we find ourselves? Should we blame those who while similar to us in appearance, hunted, captured, and profited from the sale of our ancestors? In answer I say, we must blame ourselves first; for when one accepts the blame for self-destructive behavior, only then may they hope to begin the process of repair, and recovery. No, this is not a case of "blaming the victim". To use one of your favorite biblical statements against you, I'll quote (Rev.13:10), "He that leads into captivity will go into captivity"; but what wasn't previously understood, is that it was our own ancestors Yishrayil, that by means of their refusal to serve Yah alone, that have led us this way, and since that time we have continued on that same wayward path (Lev.26:40-42). Yet in this particular case, as opposed to the time Adam blamed Him (Gen.3:12), Yah also said He'd gladly take the blame. With the practices again mentioned, Human Sacrifice, Cannibalism, Idolatry, and Paganism, Yishrayil has purposefully violated the "Blood Oath Covenant" (Ex.19-24), which was an "Unbreakable Vow", and was known to be punishable by death, and has thereby provoked His jealous nature, so much so, that the fact that we're still here alive, is indicative of the two edged sword of one, His righteous indignation, on one side, and two, His ever enduring mercy on the other. No other explanation exists for the horrors of our experiences here on one hand, and the persistence of our survival on the other; Yah is the only possible explanation.

I remember how shocked, appalled, and even nauseated I felt a few years ago when I allowed myself to see across the stream, over and beyond Denial River, that cannibalism, or at least the "make believe" version thereof, which also contains elements of "symbolic violence", all of which is sanctioned and condoned by the primary idol of Christianity; from the vault of symbolism depicted in the so-called gospels. Here's an excerpt from The Gospel According to Matthew, 26:26-28:

As they were eating, Jesus took bread, and after blessing and braking it; he gave some to the disciples saying, "Take, eat; this is my body". He took a cup, gave thanks, and gave it to them saying, "Drink all of it; for this is my blood of the covenant, which is poured out for the remission of sins".

Not only is this an abomination (Lev.17:10-14), but it is also a blasphemous mockery of the Blood Oath Covenant between Yah and the children of Yishrayil (Ex.19-24). This is also the reason that the Spanish were so easily able to convert the native South and Central Americans to Catholic Christianity. Instead of the literal, physical human sacrificing that the Aztec, Inca, and Mayans had been perfecting for centuries, the Spanish convinced them to believe that the Pope's make believe "Communion" and sacrifice in the name of, and in association with the alleged Crucifixion of Jesus Christ would more than suffice. Previously, they had been sacrificing mere mortals, but Christ was the hybridization with the immortal Creator God, which makes his sacrifice even better than that of mortal men. In this way, no one, save those drafted into, or slaughtered in opposition to their religious crusades, would actually have to die. Yes and of course, this too violates Yah's Law (Lev.17:10-14). Its also interesting to observe the pattern that these crusades most often follow. They begin under the initial pretense of kind, loving, merciful and generous "missions", but after some given period, those that refuse to "convert", or in any wise accept their chip, mark, religion, tag, or vaccine, are so mercilessly exiled, tortured and/or slaughtered "in the name of…" In this is seen confirmation of the expression, "first missionary, then mercenary".

When the children of Yishrayil were caught up in their self-inflicted desperation, they were so starved and emaciated that, instead of repentance and a return to Yah, they took matters in there own hands, and resorted to literally eating one another, and they ate their own sons and daughters, which of course was then and is now forbidden by Yah. That's right Yishrayil; I'm talking to you, about you. What do you have to brag about? So proud of yourselves for being "chosen", but our having been chosen had absolutely nothing to do with any merit on our part. In-fact our having been chosen exacerbates our level of guilt and shame. Our having been descended from such human beings as Abraham, Yitzkhaq, and Yaaqob contains no method of exultation above any others. Remember Abraham, as his name is defined, fathered many nations, and many times Yah has said that we and our ancestors have behaved far worse than the other nations; even worse than the Heathen. Would you make Yah a liar? Are we not guilty? Are we not in desperate need of repentance? Are we not in desperate need of a savior? Have we not made of ourselves cannibals and idolaters? And here we are, after all that we've been through; after all of our captivities, you still refuse to let go of your idols Yishrayil. Yah and Yah alone is our savior, but Yah has never been quite enough for you Yishrayil. Insatiable; you always need more. You always want to be, "like all the nations" (1 Sam 8:5 & 20). It's not enough to say Yah alone is our Savior. It's not enough to say Yah alone is our King. You've got to have Yah and something or someone else. You've got to have Yah and a factitious Son. Having given away; having forsaken; not realizing; forgetting that you, Oh Yishrayil, are The Son of Yah, even His first born (Ex.4:22).

2. Human Sacrifice

Human Sacrifice is forbidden throughout the Torah and Tanakh, Bible, also known as The Hebrew Scripture, but was so prevalent in the days of Abraham, that he didn't even hesitate to prepare to perform it when "tested" and commanded to do so by Yah; it was not a foreign concept (Gen.22:1-24). Surely he must have experienced an emotional relief, when as has been recorded for us in the eleventh and twelfth verses of Barashiyth; the twenty-second degree, it was revealed to him, that he had passed the test of his faith, and as it would be in the worship of Molech, or any of the other gods of war, he was not required to sacrifice his wife Sharah's first and only son, Yitzkhaq. By viewing the scriptural references listed here, or citing others of their own, all may see for themselves that previous to this occasion, and from this point forward, throughout the Torah, and the writings of the prophets, human sacrifice is emphatically forbidden.

Leviticus 18:21

"You must not let any of your children be burned as a sacrifice in the fire of Molech; you must not profane the name of Yahuwah in this way: I am Yahuwah".

Leviticus 20:1-5

Yahuwah spoke to Mosheh saying, "You must tell the children of Yishrayil, whosoever sacrifices their children to Molech must certainly be put to death. I will be against that person; the people of the land must stone him with stones. I will cut off from among their people all those who have given their child to Molech, a practice that defiles my sanctuary, and profanes My Holy Name. If the people of the land falsely claim ignorance of such behavior, and do not kill the perpetrators, then I will also be against those willfully ignorant, against their family, and will cut them off along with all that worship Molech, from among their people".

Deuteronomy 12:29-32

When Yahuwah your Father cuts off the nations that dwelt in the land before you, take heed to yourselves so that you are not ensnared by following them after they have been destroyed. Do not enquire about the methods by which they worshiped or served their gods, and then think to do likewise. You must not worship Yahuwah your Father in those ways; for every abomination that Yahuwah hates is what they have done in order to serve their gods; for even their sons and their daughters they have burnt in the fire to their gods. Simply do what I command you to without adding nor diminishing from it.

Deuteronomy 18:9-12

When you come into the land which Yahuwah your Father is giving you, you must not copy the abominable practices of those nations. There must never be found among you any one that makes their son or his daughter pass through the fire, that uses divination, an observer of times, an enchanter, a witch, a charmer, a consultant of familiar spirits, a wizard, or a necromancer; for all that do these things are an abomination to Yahuwah, and because of these abominations Yahuwah your Father is driving them away from you.

2 Kings 16:1-4

In the seventeenth year of Paqakh the son of Ramalyahuw, Ahaz the son of Yutham king of Yahuwdah began to reign. Ahaz was twenty years old when he began to reign, and reigned sixteen years in Yarushaluwm, and did that which was not right by Yahuwah Our Mighty-one, like David his father, but instead walked in the way of the wicked kings of Yishrayil, yea, and made his son to pass through the fire, according to the abominations of the heathen, whom Yahuwah had cast out from before the children of Yishrayil, and he sacrificed and burnt incense in the high places (of worship), and on the hills, and under every green tree.

When we read of the acts of Dawiyd, we see that he did several things that we would rightfully call, morally indecent. He lied, cheated, stole, committed adultery and murder. It was even implied that he may have committed a sexual act that I will not here name, but it is certain that David was a man; a real man; with faults, flaws, character defects, and short-comings like every other man. He made many mistakes in his life. He did many things that should not have been done, yet Yah called him, "a man after my own heart" (1 Sam.13:14). This is because of the one thing that David did perfectly; and it's the same thing that Yah is asking of us today, that is, he never worshiped anyone nor anything other than Yahuwah. It is David that is accredited with writing most of the psalms that we have preserved for us:

Psalm 106:34-41

They did not destroy the nations as Yahuwah had commanded them, but were mingled among the heathen, and learned their ways. They served their idols, which were a snare to them. Yea, they sacrificed their sons and their daughters to devils, and shed innocent blood, even the blood of their sons and of their daughters, whom they sacrificed to the idols of Kanaan, and the land was polluted with blood. Thus were they defiled with their own works (self-inflicted wounds), and went whoring with their own (make believe) inventions. Therefore the wrath of Yahuwah was kindled against His people. He came to abhor His own inheritance, and He gave them into the hand of the heathen; and they that hated them ruled over them.

Yeremyah, Jeremiah 19:4-7

Because they have forsaken Me, and have estranged this place, and have burned incense in it to the elohiym, whom neither they nor their fathers have known (Abraham, Yitzkhaq, Yaaqob/Yishrayil, Mosheh; none of them ever heard the name of Jesus, who was supposedly a hybrid; part god part man;

god-man, and the only Yahawashi that Mosheh knew of was his own apprentice, Bin Nuwn, who led the children of Yishrayil into the promised land after Mosheh's death. As it is written in the book of his name sake, Yahawashi (Joshua): the twenty-fourth chapter; the thirty-first verse; Yishrayil served Yahawah all the days of Yahawashi, and all the days of the elders that lived beyond Yahawashi, and which had known all the works that Yahawah had done for Yishrayil. Neither Yishrayil), nor the kings of Yahuwdah, and have filled this place with the blood of innocents (Psychopathy). They have also built the high places of Baal (The Son of The Lord Al, El; also known as Anlil, Enlil. Baal's mother was Ashtar, Ishtar, Easter; these were a trinity worshiped in Mesopotamia, Shumar, Er and Babylon), to burn their sons with fire for burnt offerings to Baal, which I never commanded, neither came into my mind. Therefore, behold, the days come, says Yah, that this place will no more be called Topheth, nor The valley of Bin Hinnom, but The valley of slaughter. I will make void the counsel of Yahuwdah and Yarushaluwm in this place, and I will cause them to fall by the sword before their enemies, and by the hands of them that seek their lives, and their carcasses will I give to be meat for the fowls of the air, and for the beasts of the earth.

Yahazaqal, Ezekiel 23:36-40

Yahuwah said to me, "Son of man, will you judge Ahalah and Ahalibah? Yea, declare to them their abominations; that they have committed adultery, and blood is in their hands, and with their idols have they committed adultery, and have also caused their sons, whom they bore me, to pass them through the fire, to devour them. Moreover this they have done to me: they have defiled my sanctuary in the same day, and have profaned my shabbaths. For when they had slain their children to their idols, then they came the same day into my sanctuary to profane it; and they did this all in My house. Furthermore, that you have sent for gurus, men to come from afar, to whom a messenger was sent; and, they came: for whom you washed yourselves, painted your eyes, and decked yourselves with ornaments (By modern western standards, this seems gay, but in many ancient cultures, it was not only socially acceptable, but highly fashionable for wealthy aristocrats to wear make-up).

Of course there are many other scriptural references that could be listed here, but one will never find a single word where Yah condoned human sacrifices. To the contrary, what one will find is exactly how much He despises this abominable practice. Human sacrifice was not merely practiced by the pagan nations as they worshiped their gods, but it was perfected by the centuries of skilled artisan priests of the craft, who passed down their knowledge by means of occult rites. Christians are kept so ignorantly of this, that they brag of the abomination of John 3:16, which says, "For God so loved the world, that he gave his only begotten Son, that whosoever believes in him should not perish, but have everlasting life", but since we can see through scripture study how human sacrifice is strictly forbidden by our creator, how can we reconcile the crucifixion, or rather "cross-of-fiction" attributed to the Christ of the "New Test"? Here's how the Christian apologists very authoritatively explain it:

"Jesus is God in the flesh. God came down as a man to die for the sins of the world. Only the blood of God is good enough to die for the world. He had to be fully man to die for man, and He had to be fully God, because only God is good enough. Man, prophet, or angel cannot die for the sins of the world. Only God in the flesh can reconcile you to God. Jesus willfully sacrificing His own life because He loved you, is not the same as these evil practices. Always remember three divine persons make up one God. The father, son Jesus, and the Holy Spirit all make up one God, the Trinity."

Again they say, "Jesus is God in the flesh"; this implies that God, previous to this miraculous event, was not flesh, but spirit, but then they say, "God came down as a man to die for the sins of the world, because only **the blood of God**" (?) Wait; blood of God? Would a truly "All-Mighty Spirit" be dependent upon the blood of an anatomical circulatory system? Do spirits even have blood? To be clear; no; spirits don't have DNA. Jesus is, in obedience to the very first commandment (Gen.1:22, 28), supposed to be a continuation of the genetic bloodline of Abraham (Gen.13:14-16). "Only the blood of God is good enough to **die** (? mortality?) for the world. He had to be fully man to die for man, and he had to be fully God, because only God is good enough" (total confusion). "Man, prophet, or angel cannot die for the sins of the world" (Deut.24:16 shows that no one can die for anyone else. If not for the unfathomable mercy of Yah, every sinner would have to die for themselves). "Only God in the flesh can reconcile you to God. Jesus, committing suicide, willfully sacrificing his own life, because he loves you, is not the same as these (even they call it) **evil practices**." They further encourage us to, "remember that three divine persons make up one God" (this clarifying the limitations of the individual facets of this three-part God). "The father" (Al, El, God, Rah, etc.), "son" (Baal, Horus, Jesus, Tammuz, etc.), and the "Holy Spirit" (Amen, Set, etc.) "all make up one God, the Trinity." All this was taught and believed by the Egyptians, Babylonians, Persians and various other peoples of the world, thousands of years before The Christ of The New Test is alleged to have been born.

As minks are bred for their skins, so desperate was He, the spirit named God, being unable to find a worthy sacrifice among men, resorted to using His own DNA (but spirits don't have DNA), in combination with that of a human virgin (Deut.22:23,24), in order to breed a hybrid to serve that sole purpose? The act of intentionally creating a Problem, in anticipation of a predictable Reaction, merely for the purpose of providing the Solution, contains a level of dishonesty that is depraved, and inconsistent with the character of an honorable being, most particularly one that we ought worship and serve. The entire premise would've been totally foreign to the patriarchs of Yishrayil, and prophets of Yah, yet this is sadly what Christians fantastically believe and teach, but this too is a violation of Yah's Law. If any of this were possible, a DNA test would prove this god-man was not "fully man", but a sort of hybrid mixture of terrestrial and extraterrestrial genetics, which was one of the many complaints held against the antediluvian god-men, also known as Nephiliym in the days of Nuwakh (Gen.6:1-9). Nuwakh's genealogy was well known and easily traced back to Adam. With no subsequent extraterrestrial hybridization, Nuwakh was fully human. The claim that Jesus was the product of a human mother and an extraterrestrial being; a Holy Ghost or angel, and that encounter being of questionable, possibly fornicative insinuation. The tale as recorded in Matthew chapter one, and Luke chapter one and three, are themselves violations of the law as recorded in Deuteronomy 22:23,24. Why would Yah violate His own law just to immaculately conceive a child, when the old copulative method works so well? Then if you flip the page to Deuteronomy 24:16, you see that no one can die for anyone else's sins; the perpetrator alone must be held accountable for his or her own sin. No one can die for your sins but you. It is Yah's boundlessly enduring mercy that saves (Psalm 136). That's it, but under the influence and indoctrination of "Churchianity", you simply can't believe that it could be just that simple.

Through the study of the acts of Qayiyn and Habiyl, two opposing characteristics of human psychological motivation are revealed; Empathy and Psychopathy. Empathy; meaning to feel for others based on a level of experience. Unlike Sympathy were we look down from aloft and say, "ah poor thing", but where for example, someone might share with you the distress of experiencing a flat tire while driving, and you having experienced the same, say to them, "I know exactly how you feel; that same thing happened to me!" Instead of looking down on the other person, we stand eye to eye; and see analogously on the same level. According to this definition, I consider myself an empath, which again explains my motivation for writing this pamphlet. All of such as opposed to Psychopathy, where the psychopath emotionally feels none of this. The psychopath, being emotionally anesthetized, can kill by means of murder of the innocent, and as a result, feel no emotional pain, no sorrow, no guilt, remorse or shame. Such was the case when Qayiyn killed his brother Habiyl. Not only did he feel no regret for the murder of his brother, but according to scripture, he actually felt justified. He thought it was a good thing, and that, "it served him right".

I explain this hoping to help the reader understand the motivation behind the worship of gods like Molech. It is only natural for those of us who struggle to comprehend the reason that a person would sacrifice their own son or daughter in the ways earlier explained, and the answer is, to intentionally produce psychopathy. If one intentionally kills his own son or daughter, even their first born, why then, at conclusion of the grieving process, would he have any feelings for the loss of another person's son, daughter, or anyone else for that matter? The worship of Molech, or any of the other war gods, is for the sole purpose of deprogramming the natural tendency of most to feel and express empathy, and to reprogram that with psychopathy. So you have forms of psychopathy; the natural born, and those that participate in such practices that do so because they believe it strengthens their resolve to better battle their enemies. Many world leaders of the past and present, such as those of the Bilderberge Group, the Trilateral Commission, and the World Economic

Forum, meet annually at various Diasporic resorts, and practice similar exercises, like that known as "The Death of Care"; the principle in-which is found the explanation of the controlled demolition of the twin towers, and that of Building 7, which was untouched by any plane, fuel, or debris on September the eleventh, 2001, yet, like the twin towers, it too fell into its own foot print, self-evident of all being an inside job, to which the sacrifice of two thousand, nine hundred and seventy-seven human lives are attributed. This number is reduced numerologically to seven, which is symbolic of completion. Evidence of which was removed and replaced by monuments dedicated to the event previous to any thorough forensic examination, so as to conceal and prevent the identification of the true perpetrators. Psychopathy also explains how and why rulers rarely hesitate to send the children of the poor into the fires of perpetual war.

You have just read how Yah repetitively and mercifully commanded our ancestors not to attempt to worship Him utilizing the same practices of those who worshiped the elohiym/gods, but the children of Yishrayil did so irregardless, and so do Christians, Messianics to this very day. Yes this does explain the historicity of our many captivities, including the one in-which we find ourselves today. It is an evolved form of servitude, that while preferable to its predecessor, we having never experienced anything better in our life-time, can only compare our present struggle to that of the relatively recent past, which is almost unanimously agreed to have been much worse. Therefore many may believe this to be "freedom", when the truth is; none are more enslaved than those, while under the control of another government, yet believe themselves free. In contrast, true freedom is when we live peacefully and securely in our own sovereign land. Once in a while we actually need to see the swastika, confederate flag, and similar symbolism in order to be reminded of the fact that, though our supposed citizenship here in this land is the only tangible reality of our present experience, we are not truly "at home". The truth is; we were all born and raised on a spiritual, mental, monetary, debt-slave plantation.

3. Idolatry

Leviticus 26:1-46

"You must not make idols for yourselves or erect an image or pillar, and you must not set up a carved stone in your land to bow down to it, for I am Yahuwah your Power. You must keep my Sabbaths and reverence my sanctuary: I am Yahuwah. If you walk in my statutes and observe my commandments and do them, then I will give you your rains in their season, and the land will yield its increase, and the trees of the field will yield their fruit. Your threshing will last to the time of the grape harvest, and the grape harvest will last to the time for sowing. You will eat your food to satiation, and dwell securely in your land.

Please continue to read and acquire this vital degree of law. Verse 1-13 spell out the blessings of righteous worship, and verses 14-46 the curses of disobedience that have surely befallen us. You can also read in the book of Shemoth, Exodus 20:1-17, which is The Ten Commandments, the second of which forbids the creation of any carved or molded images, created for the purpose of worshiping or bowing down to (Ex.20:4-7); this includes all the statues of Jesus, Mary, and Joseph, Jesus's disciples, all the saints, and The Cross as well. All of these are idols and as such are forbidden to be possessed or utilized by Yah's people.

Even I myself was a (Dick-on{hard}) Deacon; yes and was (dedicated, devoted, very devout) deep up in the cooch (church). On one particular occasion, during a procedure known as an "alter call", in which the Pastor (Bastard) would invite anyone with problems, worries, concerns, and/or "burdens" to figuratively "bring them all forward, and lay them at the foot of The Cross"; it was as if this inanimate object, or its corresponding mystical relationship to "The LORD God, Jesus, and The Holy Ghost", could actually alleviate any pain. It was a gigantic wooden cross located to the adjacent right of the podium, toward which he'd gracefully gesture. By itself it had to be 9 or 10 feet tall, but it loomed even taller as it stood up on the 4 foot stage, and on special occasions they'd even go so far as to cloak it with a white, scarlet or purple cloth. Today I actually find the practice of clothing this inanimate object to be a bit of a very sadly tragic comedy from which no one has ever been able to actualize any logical sense; unless that is, we're supposed to pretend, make-believe that Jesus left it there after his Ascension?

On this particular day I accepted the call as I had done many times before, in fact I recall being pleased to participate, and even looked forward to the ceremony, but this time was different. This time was as if a blind fold had been removed, and I was allowed to see; to be consciously aware of the violation in conflict with scriptural law, and it nagged me incessantly. I went up front nevertheless, and to the Deacon that coincidentally knelt next to me (as the many members of the congregation knelt there together), while the Pastor initiated his prayer, I foolishly whispered asking, "You know how the 10 Commandments forbid bowing down to and worshiping carved images (Ex.20:4-7)?" When he answered in the affirmative I said, "Well that giant cross on the stage in front of us is just such an image, and here we are bowing beneath it." He then looked up at the cross and back at me and said, "Only devils have a problem with the Cross." I asked, "How can I be a devil when I'm kneeling down here next to you?" Though I didn't say it to him, truth is that; only the willfully ignorant, or those in denial of scriptural truth, regardless of their motives, bow to carved images. Needless to say, that was the end of that conversation, and if I recall correctly it was the last time I attended that church; after having been active in weekly attendance there for several years. It was a day or so later that I got a call from the assistant Pastor who said that he had heard that I had some questions. I agreed and actually took the time to gather my notes, and after having asked several questions about carved images, dietary laws, ethnic significance, pagan holidays, etc., which we discussed at length, he eventually admitted having no clear answers as to why various denominations, his included, maintained these practices contrary to scriptural law.

Exodus 32:1-10

When the people noticed Mosheh's extended stay on the mount, the people gathered themselves to meet with Aharon, and said to him, "Let's make gods for ourselves, which will go before us; for as for this Mosheh, the man that brought us up out of the land of Egypt (It was actually Yah that had done this), we have no idea what has become of him. Aaron said, "Take off the golden earrings that are in the ears of your wives, of your sons, and of your daughters, and bring them to me". And all the people took off the golden earrings which were in their ears, and brought them to Aharon (This proves that wearing jewelry is no sin). He received them at their hand, and with an engraving tool, he fashioned the molten medal, making it into a calf: and they said, "This O Yishrayil, represents the (trinity of) gods that brought you up out of the land of Egypt". When Aharon saw their zeal and pleasure, he built an altar before it; and Aharon proclaimed, "Tomorrow is a feast to Yahuwah" (confusion and philosophical hybridization inspired by pretension and make-believe). And they rose up early on the next day, and offered burnt offerings, and brought peace offerings; and the people sat down to eat and to drink, and rose up to play.

Yahuwah said to Mosheh, "Get back down to the people that you brought out of the land of Egypt; they have corrupted themselves: In the short time that has elapsed, they have turned aside out of the way which I commanded them: they have made themselves a molten calf, and have worshiped it, and have sacrificed to it, and said, These are your gods, O Yishrayil, which have brought you up out of the land of Egypt. I have studied these people, and as anyone may see, they are an especially hardheaded, stiff-necked and rebellious strain: Now leave me alone so that I may destroy them, and then I will make of you a great nation. It was just after this occasion that Mosheh actually offered to sacrifice himself for the sins of the children of Yishrayil, but Yah refused his offer (Deuteronomy 32:32,33).

Go ahead and read the rest of that degree of law and see where instead of accepting Yah's offer to make of him a great nation, Mosheh bargained to spare the lives of our ancestors who we continue to mimic even to this day; as yet still clambering to worship The Trinitarian God of Father/Rah, Son/Horus/Jesus, and Holy Ghost/Amen, thinking of this as the right way to worship Yahuwah, instead of simply worshiping him in the way in which He commanded.

Oh yeah, and concerning The Worship of The Son, whether you call him Adab, Adonis, Alcides, Atys, Baal, Bali, Beddru, Bin Hadar, Buddha, Bremhilla, Cadmus, Ceita, Christ, Deva, Esos, Fo, Gentaut, Horus, Hesus, Hil, Indra, Isa, Ixion, Jao, Jesus, Joshua, Krishna, Logos, Mithra, Mikado, Odin, Osiris, Prometheus, Qirinius, Quaxacote, Salivahana, Tai, Teta, Thammuz, Thor, Tien, Tschy, Wittoba, Xamotis, Yahawashi, Yahuwashi, Yahwashi, Yahshua, Yaut, Yeshua, Yesus, Zeus, Zoab, Zoroaster, or any other derivative of that name or position of authority, the narrative and dilemma surrounding it remains the same. Whether we're considering the fact that they were all born of a virgin, or some other miraculous method of conception, on the 25th of December, fed the poor, heeled the sick, resurrected the dead, were causelessly hated and crucified, or killed by some other means, and was resurrected three days after, etc. The most accurate and valued usage of the name Yahawashi, Yahuwashi, Yahwashi, Yahshua, Yeshua, Yesus, Joshua, in Hebrew Scripture is rightly applied to Mosheh's apprentice, who took over the duties of leadership after the departure of Mosheh, leading the children of Yishrayil into the promised land (Deuteronomy, chapter 34, verses 9 &10). After the Torah, which is the first five books of your Bible and of the Hebrew Scripture, the very next book is named after him; that is Yahuwashi, but he is not Hamashiyakh, The Christ that you've been expecting to "return" for the past 2000 years (Matthew, chapter16, verses 27 & 28).

Let's take another brief look at the "New Test", to see how you've continued the maintenance of this inordinate form of worship. One of the greatest ironies contained therein is located in the book of Matthew, chapter 4, verse 8-10; during the episode in-which the Christ of the New Testament is being tempted by his archenemy, a character named Satan. In his response to the third and final of such temptations, specifically dealing with the question of appropriate subjects of worship, in order to repel the tempter, in a severe case of irony, he quotes from the Torah:

8. Again, the devil took him up into an exceeding high mountain, and showed him all the kingdoms of the world, and the glory of them;

9. And said to him, All these things will I give you, if you will fall down and worship me.

10. Then said Jesus to him, Get away Satan: for it is written, You must worship the Lord your God, and **him only must you serve.**

Compare this to the sentiment of the Torah; Dabariym, Deuteronomy; the sixth degree: verses five, and twelve through sixteen, which is what the redactors of the "New Test" are alluding to. Yet while you, the reader, even while engrossed in the narrative of the myth, are thereby being tempted to participate in an inordinate form of worship, paraphrasing the correct sentiment, Jesus is alleged to have not fallen prey to such temptation.

Even-though there are many more examples I could cite, in the interest of time, I'm only going to draw one verse from each of the four good-spells respectively, in order to illustrate just how "good" a "spell" has been cast upon the Messianics.

Matthew 28, verse 9
And as they went to tell his disciples, behold, Jesus met them, saying, All hail. And they came and held him by the feet, and worshiped him.

Mark 5, verse 6
But when he saw Jesus afar off, he ran and worshiped him,

Luke 24, verse 52
And they worshiped him, and returned to Jerusalem with great joy:

John 9, verse 38
And he said, Lord, I believe. And he worshiped him.

All violations of The Law, according to which, O Yishrayil, as Jesus told Satan, we are to worship no one nor anything other than Yahawah & Yahawah alone. You have taken the blond haired, blue eyed, pale skinned Jesus that was forced upon us, and having remade him in our own image, and having changed his name to Yahawashi, now believe that the worship of this person is acceptable. In reference to scriptural principles like that of Deut.6:5, the question remains: What is the definition of the word "**ALL**"?

Deut.6:5, 12-16

You must love Yahuwah your Father with **all** your heart, and with **all** your soul, and with **all** your might.

Once again I could choose from among many scriptural references to prove this point (Deut.6:12-18), but one of my favorites is:

Deut.10:12-22

Now, Yishrayil, what does Yahuwah require of you, but to revere Yahuwah, to walk in **all** His ways, and to love him, and to serve Yahuwah with **all** your heart and with **all** your soul (how do you define the word "**all**"?), to keep the commandments of Yahuwah, and His statutes, which I command you this day for your good? Look, the entire earth and everything therein belongs to Yahuwah, but Yahuwah desired to love your forefathers, and he chose their seed after them, even you (the seed of Abraham, Yitzkhaq, Yaaqob/Yishrayil) above all people, as it is this day. Therefore I erg you to circumcise the foreskin of your heart, and don't be stiff-necked anymore; for Yahuwah your Father is **King of kings**, and Ruler of rulers, a great Power, mighty and terrible, Who shows no partiality of persons, nor receiver of bribes or rewards: He executes judgment of the fatherless and widow, and loves the stranger, in giving him food, shelter and clothing. Empathize with the foreigner: for you too were foreigners in the land of Egypt. Respect Yahuwah; **Him alone must you serve, and to Him alone you must cleave and swear by His Name alone.** He is your praise, and he is your Power, that has done for you these great and terrible things, which your eyes have seen. Your fathers went down into Egypt with threescore and ten persons; and now Yahuwah has made you as the stars of heaven for multitude (Gen.13:14-16).

Repetitively I ask, "What is your definition of the word "**ALL**"? The dictionary definition leaves no wiggle room for the worship of anyone or anything other than Yah & Yah alone. Yet this has rarely been enough for you

Yishrayil; to this day you can't even fathom the worship of Yah alone. You have to have someone or something in association with Yah, as if He alone is not enough; He has to have His Son tag along in order to assist Him, and to assist you in your desire for an alternative Savior. Look here at the example of Manashshah Bin Khazaqiyah Bin Yahuwdah Bin Yishrayil. Though he was a son of one of the most righteous kings of Yishrayil, he was one of the most wicked.

2 Kings 21:1-26

Manasseh was twelve years old when he began to reign, and (out of love and appreciation for Khazaqiyah, Yahawah allowed) he (Manashshah to) reigned fifty-five years in Jerusalem. His mother's name was Hephzibah. He did what is evil in the sight of Yahuwah, according to the despicable practices of the nations whom Yahuwah drove out before the people of Yishrayil. He rebuilt the high places (of worship, i.e. churches, mosques, and temples) that Khazaqiyah his father had destroyed, and he erected altars for **Baal,** (which is the same as The Lord, Jesus), and made an Asherah (The Cross), as Ahab king of Yishrayil had done, and worshiped all the host of heaven and served them. He also built altars in The House of Yahuwah, of which Yahuwah had said, "In Yabuwshaluwm will I put My Name." He built altars for all the host of heaven in the two courtyards of the house of, Bayith Yahuwah; this means that not only was Manasseh mindful and studious of Zodiology, but he also had priests who sacrificed to each of the twelve respective deities along with their attending parishioners (and he had the nerve to do all this at the same temple that Shaluwman had built for The Name of Yahuwah).

In closing this portion, I want to take another look at the primary idol of the Christian religion, namely Jesus Christ. According to the narrative of this story, which is ruminated in three of the four good-spells, Jesus was in the midst of a lecture, when someone interrupted the meeting with an urgent message from his mother, Mary. In a rant of great irreverence, this person is reported to have disowned his own mother and brethren with the following rhetoric:

Matt 12:48 & 49

But he answered and said unto him that told him, Who is my mother? and who are my brethren? And he stretched forth his hand toward his disciples, and said, Behold my mother and my brethren!

Mark 3:33 & 34

And he answered them, saying, Who is my mother, or my brethren? And he looked round about on them which sat about him, and said, Behold my mother and my brethren!

Luke 8:21

And he answered and said unto them, My mother and my brethren are these which hear the word of God, and do it.

Ironically, those who truly hear, understand, and obey the word of Yah, actually worship Yah & Yah alone, but instead, this is the kind of person we want to hold up as our leader? The objective here, is to impress the reader with the zeal that this man was demonstrating to his listeners. There was a time when even I expected that all should follow such a one who would disrespect his own mother before a live audience, but to the contrary, Yahuwah's Law commands us to "honor our father and mother" (Ex.20:12, number 5 of the 10 Commandments). Oh Yishrayil, we are an especially hardheaded, stiff-necked, rebellious, and idolatrous strain. Had any other nation witnessed the works Yah did before the eyes of our fathers, surely they'd have worshiped Him, and Him alone.

The book of Shamath, Shemoth, Exodus; the twentieth degree contains the so-called, "Ten Commandments". The first two most specifically counter idolatry, and thus pertain intimately to present subject matter, so I will limit this discussion to them. The others, though equally as pertinent, require more protracted explanation that could potentially take the conversation in other directions.

Number 1:

1 Yahuwah spoke all these words, saying,
2 I am Yahuwah of the Elohiym, which have brought you out of the land of Mitzrahiym, out of the state of slavery.
3. You must have no hinder gods before me.

Number 2:

4 You must not use any man-made image, or any likeness of any thing that is in heaven above, or that is in the earth beneath,
or that is in the water under the earth:
5 You must not bow down to them, nor serve them: for I Yahuwah am jealous, visiting the iniquity of the fathers upon the
children to the third and fourth generation of them that hate me;
6 And showing mercy to thousands of them that love me, and keep my commandments.

While I continue to hope for the progress of our awakening, and that this should be our last, it is most certainly not the first of our captivities. Our ancestors were slaves in Egypt, then mercifully freed by Yah; Babylon, then freed; Persia, then freed; Greece, then freed; Rome, then freed; and all for the exact same reason we are in this captivity today. When the children of those that purchased and brought our ancestors here in slave ships and chains say that, now that they are finished with us, we are free to go, where will we go Yishrayil? Will we go "back to Africa", as if the Khamitic children of those who sold us should care? They worship the same idols there, as fervently as they that worship them here.

I've heard you say that you are tired of this existence under a racist people that hate us because of the color of our skin, but I promise you, that though the Khamitic may not hate us for the color of our skin; whether its religion, language, culture, family lineage, or any other, they eventually find reasons to hate, lie to, and if we go there with, or in time acquire possessions, in one way shape or form, they will steal them. They have no reason to love us; why should they care? Many of them are Muslim, and greet us saying, "As-salamu alaykum", "Peace upon you", but is this greeting sincere? Is it possible to have a true and lasting peace with someone that worships anyone other than Yahuwah? Don't you know that Arabic is simply another slave master's tongue? What makes that master's tongue, better than this master's tongue? The one and only Master of a free Yishrayiliy ought to be Yah & Yah alone. It was by freedom of choice that our fathers agreed to accept the principles of the covenant with Yahawah. It was by freedom of choice that we've violated said covenant, and by freedom of choice must we return to the worship of Yah & Yah alone. If we are rightly perceived as "herd animals", then Yahuwah is our shepherd (Psalm 23); He spoke to our forefathers in our native Hebraic tongue, of which we ought to at least begin to acquire some basic fundamental knowledge; beginning with something as simple as, the history of the letter "J".

4. Messy Genealogy

First of all, let's start by reviewing some of the scriptural references in which we all agree, and then later I'll reveal those by which I had initially been troubled:

One thing that all Messianic prophecies share in common concerning Hamashiyakh, The Messiah, The Christ, The Anointed, The One, is that he must be descended from Malik Dawiyd, King David. For the sake of memory refreshment,   let's read Yahazaqal, Yechetzqyah, Ezekiel: the thirty-forth chapter; the twenty-third verse as a first example.

23. I will set up one shepherd over them, and he will feed them – My servant Dawiyd; he will feed them, and he will be their shepherd.

Yahazaqal, Ezekiel: the thirty-seventh chapter; verses fifteen to twenty-eight.

21. And say to them, "This is what Yah, The Sovereign says; Behold, I will take the children of Yishrayil from among the heathen, from wherever they are, and will gather them from every part of the earth, and bring them into their own land.
22. And I will make them one nation in the land of Yishrayil; and one will be king over all of them: they will no longer be two nations, nor will they be divided into two kingdoms (respectively that is; Ahalah and Ahalibah, Messianic and Orthodox, Blue and Red, Liberal and Conservative, Left and Right, North and South, Yishrayil and Yahuwdah):
23. Never again will they defile themselves with their idols, nor with their detestable things, nor with any of their transgressions: but I will save them wherever they dwell, and in whatever ways they have sinned I will cleanse them: so will they be my people, and I will be their Power.

24. And Dawiyd my servant will be king over them; and they all will have one shepherd: they will also walk in my judgments, and observe my statutes, and do them.

25. And they will dwell in the land that I have given to Yaaqob my servant; and they will dwell in the same land wherein their fathers dwelt; they and their children, and their children's children for ever: and my servant Dawiyd will be their prince forever.

26. Moreover I will make an everlasting covenant of peace with them. I will situate them and cause them to multiply, and I'll set my sanctuary in the midst of them for evermore.

27. My personal residence will be with them: Yes, I will be their Power, and they will be My people.

28. And the heathen will know that I Yah do sanctify Yishrayil, when My sanctuary will be in the midst of them for evermore."

Now turn to Yishayahuw, Isaiah: the eleventh chapter: verses one to nine.

1. There will come forth a rod out of the stem of Yishuwah, and a Branch will grow out of his roots:

2. The spirit of Yah will rest on him, the spirit of wisdom and comprehension, the spirit of counsel and might, the spirit of knowledge and of the fear of Yah;

3. This will make him of great overstanding in the fear of Yah: and he will not judge after the sight of his eyes, neither reprove after the hearing of his ears:

4. But with righteousness will he judge the poor, and reprove with equity for the meek of the earth: and he will hit the earth with the rod of his mouth, and with the breath of his lips will he slay the wicked (This is speaking of the Spoken Word, delivered predominantly by Poetry + Music = Hip Hop, and Rap).

5. Righteousness will be the girdle of his loins, and faithfulness the girdle of his reins (Christians typically stop reading at this point because the next four verses clarify the fact that this is a yet unfulfilled prophecy).

6. The wolf also will dwell with the lamb, and the leopard will lie down with the kid; and the calf and the young lion and the fatling together; and a little child will lead them.

7. The cow and the bear will feed; their young ones will lie down together: and the lion will eat straw like the ox.

8. The nursing child will play near the hole of an asp, and the weaned child will put his hand on the viper's den.

9. They will not hurt nor destroy anything in my entire holy mountain: for the earth will be as full of the knowledge of Yah, as the waters that cover the sea.

Yaramiyah, Yeremyah, Jeremiah: the twenty-third chapter; the fifth verse.

4. "Look, now the days have come", says Yah, "that I will raise to Dawiyd a righteous Branch, and a King will reign and prosper,
and will execute judgment and justice in the earth."

Yaramiyah, Jeremiah: the thirtieth chapter; verses seven to ten.

7. "Regrettably, it is because that day is so terrible that none is like it: it is the time of Yaaqob's trouble; but he will be saved out of it.

8. It will come to pass in that day", says Yah of hosts, "that I will break the oppressor's yoke from off his neck, and will break
his chains, and strangers will no longer be served by him:

9. But they will serve Yah their Power, and Dawiyd their king, whom I will raise up to them.

10. Therefore don't be afraid My servant Yaaqob", says Yah; "neither be dismayed Yishrayil: for behold, I will save you from
afar and your seed from the land of their captivity; and Yaaqob will return, and will be in rest, and be quiet, and none will
make him afraid".

Yaramiyah, Jeremiah: the thirty-third chapter; verses fourteen to seventeen.

14. "Behold, the days come", says Yah, "that I will perform that great thing that I have promised to the house of Yishrayil and to

the house of Yahuwdah.

15. In those days and at that time I will cause the Branch of righteousness to spring up from Dawiyd; and he will execute judgment and righteousness in the land.

16. In those days Yahuwdah will be saved, and Yerusalem will live in safety: proclaiming that Yah is Righteous".

17. for this is what Yah says, "Dawiyd will never fail to have a man sitting on the throne of the house of Yishrayil".

Okay now, you'll rarely get much of an argument against the scriptural verses we've seen thus far; as I've said before, I am a Messianic Hebrew Yishrayiliy [Later I'll explain exactly what I mean by this term;"Messianic". My definition will most likely vary from your own], but I must again warn you to strap yourself in. We are sure to encounter turbulence in the flight ahead:

As you have already seen In Yaramiyah, Jeremiah: the thirty-third chapter; verse seventeen Yah said, "Dawiyd will never fail to have a man sitting on the throne of the house of Yishrayil". Seemingly ignorant of the timeline and the **conditionality** of such statements, the writers and redactors of the Greek/Roman/Christian Bible, believing this to be a vital requirement, spent almost two chapters successfully convincing the overwhelming majority of their readers of the genealogical record of Yahawashi, Yahuwshua, whom we had previously been taught, from The King James Version, to call Jesus [even though the letter "J", incepted into English approximately 1685 CE., is still far less than four hundred years old, does not exist in Hebrew, nor did it previously exist in any other language, and there has never been any ancient Hebrew named Jesus; because Jesus is not a Hebrew name; yet we've been taught to say our prayers in that name], as being traced back to King David. However, as you are about to see, when the genealogical records, as recorded in Matthew and Luke are placed under the magnification of diligent research, we find that critical and crucial problems are revealed. Before doing so, due to the fact that so many have been kept in the dark concerning this conditionality, I perceive it necessary at this point, to clearly illustrate at least one example of the conditional nature of Yah's promises to Yishrayil, and then later I will share still others. One of many is found in First Kings: the ninth chapter; verses one to nine:

1. When Shalomon had finished building The House of Yahuwah, the king's house, and all that he desired to do,

2. Yahuwah appeared to Shalomon a second time, just as he had appeared to him at Gibeon.

3. And Yahuwah said to him, "I have heard your prayer and your supplication that you have made before me: I have hallowed this house, which you have built, to put My Name there forever; and my eyes and my heart will be there perpetually.

4. **If you will walk** before me, as Dawiyd your father walked, in integrity of heart, and in uprightness, to do according to all that I have commanded you, and will keep my statutes and my judgments (worshiping no one and nothing other than Yah):

5. **Then** I will establish the throne of your kingdom in Yishrayil forever, as I promised to Dawiyd your father, saying, "There will never fail to be a man on the throne of Yishrayil".

6. **But** if you won't follow me, you or your children, and will not keep My commandments and my statutes which I have set before you, but go and serve hinder gods, and worship them:

7. **Then** I will cut off Yishrayil out of the land which I have given them; and this house, which I have hallowed for My Name, I will cast out of my sight; and Yishrayil will be a proverb and a byword (such as African American, Black, Colored, Moore, Negro, Nigger, etc.) among all people:

8. And though this house is now exalted, every one that passes by it will be astonished, and will scoff; and ask, "Why has Yahuwah done this to this land, and to this house (to this people)?"

9. And they will answer, "Because they forsook Yahuwah their Power, who brought their fathers out of the land of Egypt, and have taken hold of hinder gods, and have worshiped them, and served them: therefore Yahuwah (not Satan, the Devil, the White Man, etc., nobody but Yahuwah) has brought all this evil upon them."

In reference to the highlighted verses above, we could end the entire discussion and here close the pamphlet, because those verses actually encompass the totality of the gist, but because I know how stubborn you are, greater clarity on the conditionality of Yah's promises to Yishrayil, is recorded in Leviticus 26 & Deuteronomy 28 in their entireties, and if it's not clear after that then I'm sure it'll require Yah's personal touch to remove your denial.

If we turn to the book of Huwashiyah, Hosea: the third chapter: verses four and five: we see that Huwashiyah would also seem to contradict Yaramiyah, Jeremiah: the thirty-third chapter; verse seventeen, where He said, "Dawiyd will never fail to have a man sitting on the throne of the house of Yishrayil".

4. For the children of Yishrayil (Twelve tribes; for JC is accredited with being the king of all Yishrayil, not just two tribes or ten tribes, but 2+10=12) will live many days without a king, without a prince, without a sacrifice, without an image, without an ephod, and without statues and images of gods.

Then verse five speaks of a reformation in the "latter days".

5. Afterward the children of Yishrayil will return, and seek Yah their Power and Dawiyd their Prince; and **in the latter days**
they will respect the righteousness of Yah.

Previous to "the latter days", spoken of in verse 5 above, Yishrayil will suffer through the self-inflicted hell on earth that was also prophesied of us. With that clarification and while Christians/Messianics "**believe**" that the ancient Hebrew prophecies speak in reference to the Christ of the "New Testament", while belief has its rightful place, it is also important to know that there are some who would take advantage of other's instinctive desire to "trust and believe"; therefore knowledge; light, the substantiation and maintenance thereof, is more reliable than blind faith and belief.

Christians often speak with braggadocio concerning the great deeds and accomplishments of their master, feeding the poor, healing the sick, exorcising demons, etc.; noble works in deed, but one thing universally undeniable is the fact that, before any of the descendants of Adam can perform any works, "good" or "bad"; since the womb is the one and only portal into this plane of existence, he or she must first be born of a woman, and this is one of the points in these Greek/Roman writings, the authors attempt to sustain.

Now being that it occurs first in the chronology of the book, our attempt at **[1 Thessalonians 5:21, where Shaul, Paul rightly encourages us to "prove all things"] substantiating** the genealogy of this Christ ought to begin by examining the writing attributed to its alleged author, Matthew. It would only be proper that we should start there; in the so-called, "Gospel" [a compound word; ghost-spell, god's-spell, "good-spell" also known as "the good story". It is in fact a magic spell, in which members of the general populous, also known as "The Sheeple", are kept ignorant of, and unwittingly submissive to, a system of governmental control; govern = control, ment = mind, al = pertaining to] According to ["according to"? Any utilization of the phrase "according to" immediately interjects doubt, as it reveals the existence of possibly viable alternatives] Saint Matthew: the first chapter; verses one to seventeen, where <u>the genealogy of Joseph</u>, who was the husband of Mary, is traced back to King David.

As we begin to read, it becomes immediately obvious that, verse one is an introductory statement, and that it is clearly designed to <u>lead its readers to "believe"</u> that they are about to learn the genealogy of Jesus Christ, since it actually states that intent word verbatim.

1. ¶ The book of the generation of Jesus Christ, the son of David, the son [seed] of Abraham.

As we continue to read, we are led verse by verse through a series of <u>begetting</u>, with emphasis on DNA matching bloodlines. However, after we've read this well-established pattern, and have been thoroughly convinced of the genealogy listed in verses one to seventeen, in verses eighteen to twenty-five Matthew himself contradicts the entire premise. After seventeen verses to the contrary, Matthew explains that Joe wasn't actually the father of Jesus. As it turns out, this is expedient in order to establish the claim that Jesus wasn't the product of a normal conception, but he was immaculately conceived by a virgin; without the use of either penis or sperm. As we all know, that would be "nasty", and we wouldn't dream of having our messiah conceived of such despicably mammalian means; right? The claim is that Mary never had sexual relations with her fiance, or any other man for that matter, previous to The Messiah's conception, and, and well; you, you see; what, what had; what had happen; what had happen was; Jesus was miraculously conceived through the "Holy Spirit". Of course this contradicts the well established fact that, if ghosts and spirits exist at all, they do so on a plane that is absent of DNA, and are therefore incapable of obeying Yah's universal commandment to all flesh (Gen.1:22,28); "Be fruitful and multiply". I parenthetically interjected the word "seed" above in order to remind the reader that it was Abraham's seed that Yah promised to multiply like the sand at the sea shore, the dust of the earth, and the stars in the sky (Gen.13:14-16). It was also David and Abraham's physical seed that was implicated in verse one above, and we've known since the beginning, that this is only made possible by the utilization of that matter known as deoxyribonucleic acid, DNA; also known as flesh. If the genealogy as recorded in the book of Matthew were valid, it might possibly trace Joe, back to King David, but because it never connects Joe as the father of Jesus, it then becomes quite clear that the genealogical record as accredited to Matthew is being used here as part of a farce, and actually has no way of establishing bloodline ascent from Jesus to David.

Finding themselves disappointed, thoroughly challenged, and frankly in a bit of a pickle consistent of this startling realization, some Christians have convinced themselves and others to "**believe**" that, even though Joe wasn't the actual biological father of Jesus, he was the legal guardian, and thereby in principle passed on his genealogical line by means of adoption. However, there are three not so easily refutable problems that exist with this response:

1) There is absolutely no mention of any record in the Christian's Bible that would indicate that Joseph actually adopted Jesus; neither does this adoption have any reference in any of the prophecies. As Amos 3:7 explains, Yah does nothing without "revealing His secret to His servants the prophets"; there is no reference in the Hebrew Scripture to any adopted messiah.

2) Even if a case for this adoption could be made, it is absolutely impossible to pass on one's genealogy by means of adoption. That was the core of Abraham's complaint to Yah when he spoke against adopting his Syrian servant Aliazar/Eliezer in the entirety of the fifteenth degree of Barashiyth; verses one through four in particular, and in His response, Yah emphatically agreed that the elderly Abraham and wife Sharah, would indeed have the physical "pleasure" of conceiving and suckling a natural born, direct blood descended, DNA matching son of their very own [Gen.15:1-4].

The Hebrew Scripture gives us many examples of how Levitical priests, for instance, starting with Aharon, were born to another **priest and his wife**. In other words, **if your father is a priest, then you may be a priest.** On the other hand, hypothetically, if a priest adopts a man-child who is the son of someone who was not a priest or Luwahiy, Levite, through adoption that child should, would, and could never become a priest. That would be illegal, immoral and unethical. The Law of Yah would be brought against him, and would successfully contest his right to either the Levitical or Zadakial Priesthood. In other words, one would have to be a direct blood descended, DNA matching Levite, in order to be accepted in the Levitical Priesthood. The Christ of the New Test would not be able to trace lineage to Aharon or Zadak and therefore could never be able to claim any part in the priesthood. The same is true for the royal lineage of the Yahuwdahiym, and even-though prophets might arise from any of the twelve tribes, Yah commanded that they had to be from among the children of Yishrayil and no other nation; certainly not another frequency, plane of existence, or planet.

3) Even if one would want to conclude and argue that through adoption the genealogy might be acceptable, an additional, deeply profound, and irrefutable problem still remains. Through study we find that in Matthew: the first chapter; the twelfth verse, Matthew [1: 11&12] traces the genealogical line of Joseph through a King named Jeconiah, aka Coniah, Yehoaikin, or Yahyakin. The problem arises in Yaramiyahuw, Yeremiyahuw, Jeremiah: the twenty-second chapter; verses twenty-four to

thirty; giving special attention to verse thirty, were it says that the ancestor of Yahsiph, Joseph named King Jeconiah, Coniah, Yehoaikin, Yahyakin was cursed by Yah:

30. This is what Yah says, "Write this man down as childless, a man that will not succeed in his lifetime; for no man of his seed will succeed in sitting on the throne of Dawiyd or ruling anymore in Yahuwdah."

Recently taking it upon myself to reread the book of Yaramiyah in its entirety, I was pleasantly reassured of his strict adherence to the orthodoxy of service to Yah alone, and now our review of the excerpted passage attached above clarifies the scriptural fact that any descendant of Jeconiah must be disqualified from ever being a Messianic candidate; and therefore, if Christians insist on making Jesus the legally adopted child of the disqualified Joseph, then it is obvious that Jesus also would be disqualified from even potentially being Almasih, Hamashiyakh, The Messiah, The Christ, The Anointed One, The Ubermensch.

After taking the necessary time to study the scripture and view what is actually written therein, many Messianics, Christians find themselves reluctantly having to concede to the fact that the genealogical acFffount attributed to Matthew must be discarded, but this then compels the thinker to ask, "How can we continue to rely on a book that has been so easily proven at the onset to begin with such a fictional account? I mean, if a story begins as a lie, mustn't it continue to be, and yet conclude as a lie?"

After having dismissed the account of The Messianic Genealogy of The Christ of The New Testament, as it was recorded in the King James version of The Gospel According to Matthew, in adherence to the precept of having a minimum of two witnesses (Deut.17: verse 6, & 19: verse 15), we ought to take the writing that has been attributed to the honorable Dr. Luke into consideration:

In an attempt to avoid these very difficult challenges, staunch Christian supporters claim that the better genealogy of Jesus can be traced back to King David through his mother, Mary. This claim is made by those considering the genealogical record found in the third book of the Greek writings, the third chapter thereof; the book of Luke; verses twenty-three to thirty-eight, which also attempts a genealogical trace back to Malik Dawiyd. Once again, there are at least three problems with this claim:

1) There is absolutely no evidence whatsoever that Luke's account of the genealogy is that of Mary. If read in either the Greek or the English of The King James Version, the chapter clearly states this to be the genealogy of Joseph. You see, in that time and locality, the social status of unmarried women was strictly based on that of her father/family; she alone having very low, if any, ranked barely above slaves. In addition to this fact, Theologians, Bible Scholars agree that Mary would also have been approximately twelve to fourteen years of age when Jesus was born, and being unwed, would have been able to make absolutely no legal claims to property ownership. With full knowledge of these facts, the male chauvinistic Roman authors of the book, writing in Greek, in order to deceptively depict, greater antiquity, didn't even so much as once mention this young woman in this very questionable genealogy. Another interesting observation frequently boasted upon in some contemporary theological schools of thought, is the social acceptability of God, The Holy Ghost, or an Angel having been "**F**ound **U**nder **C**arnal **K**nowledge" of, or otherwise "magically" impregnating such a young woman, and the contrasting sentiment that would be levied against a mortal man having been guilty of the same; he'd be judged, condemned,   and categorized among Black Magicians, Mad Scientists, Pedophiles, or Statutory Rapists to name but a few, but in their ignorance, or amnesia, they neglect to acknowledge the narrative of the story in-which Mary was said to have been engaged, and expected to soon wed a mortal man; a carpenter named Yahsiph, Joseph, who according to tradition, would likely have been no less than thirty-five years of age, as that was then, and yet remains customary in that part of the world.

2) Even if Mother Mary could trace a lineage back to Malik Dawiyd, it wouldn't help in the case of the defendant Jesus Christ, because **according to male dominated Hebrew Scripture, and contrary to Yiddish, European Jewish tradition**, though mothers are occasionally given

honorable, and sometimes dishonorable mention, family, tribal, royal, priestly affiliation, lineage, and genealogy can only be traced and verified through the person's father. We are provided with many examples of this in the Torah. It may be beneficial to examine a few of them:

For examples of **Priestly Lineage** let's start with Exodus: the twenty-eighth degree; the fourth verse.

4.   These are the garments they are to make for the High Priest; a breastplate, an ephod, a robe, a woven tunic, a turban (1 Cor.11:4), and a sash. They are to make these holy garments for your brother Aharon, and his sons, that they may serve Me as priests (no mothers, wives, sisters or daughters were here mentioned).

Exodus, Shamath, Shemoth: the twenty-ninth degree; verses nine to thirty.

9. You must clothe Aharon and his sons as I have instructed, put the caps on them (This contradicts the teachings of Paul who taught it to be a sin for a man to cover his head when praying or ministering to Yah [1 Cor.11:4], but here we see that, not only is there nothing wrong with wearing a cap, kippa, or kufi, it is actually commanded by Yah to the priests), and <u>The Priesthood will be theirs as a perpetual statute.</u> In this way, you will consecrate Aharon and his sons.

10. Bring a bull to the front of the Tent of Meeting: Aharon and his sons must put their hands on the head of the bull.

15. You must also take one ram; and Aharon and his sons will put their hands on the head of the ram.

19. And you must take the other ram; and Aharon and his sons will put their hands on the head of the ram.

20. Then you must kill the ram, and take of his blood, and put it on the tip of the right ear of Aharon, and on the tip of the right ear of his sons, and on the thumb of their right hand, and on the great toe of their right foot, and sprinkle some of the blood on and around the altar (The New Testament book of Hebrews: the ninth chapter alleges that instead of using the blood of animals in his sacrifice, JC used his own, which in itself is a violation of Yah's Law. However, the exact nature of this sacrifice has been omitted from the explanation. What are the exact mechanics? The Devil is in the details. How exactly was this sacrifice carried out? Exactly how was the blood drawn and utilized? Did he have to cut his fingers or toes? Was his jugular vein and carotid artery

severed by Shakhat as is prescribed in animal sacrifice and consumption? Was the blood collected in a basin, mixed with water and sprinkled on the heavenly altar with a hyssop brush? By what means was it sprinkled upon the people in order to bring them into this, "New Covenant"? If you say that it was by means of "The Cross", then again you will have to show where the prophets of Yah spoke of this. Which one of the prophets said that a cross, tree, or stake would replace or substitute for Shakhat?).

21. You must take of the blood that is on the altar, and the **anointing oil**, and sprinkle it on Aharon, on his sons, and on all of their garments: and in this way they and their garments will be hallowed.

24. You must put all in the hands of Aharon and in the hands of his sons; and must wave them for a wave offering before Yah.

26. You must take the breast of the ram of Aharon's consecration, and wave it for a wave offering before Yah: and it will be your part.

27. You must sanctify the breast of the wave offering, and the shoulder of the heave offering, which is waved, and which is heaved up, of the ram of the consecration, even of that which is for Aharon, and of that which is for his sons:

28. It will be Aharon's and his son's by a statute forever from the children of Yishrayil: for it is a heave offering: and it will be a heave offering from the children of Yishrayil of the sacrifice of their peace offerings to Yah.

29. The holy garments of Aharon will be his son's after him, to be **anointed** and consecrated therein.

30. That son that is priest in his stead will put them on seven days, when he comes into the tabernacle of the congregation to minister in the holy place.

Exodus, Shamath, Shemoth: the thirtieth degree; verse thirty.

30. You must **anoint** Aharon and his sons, and consecrate them, that they may serve me as priests.

Exodus, Shamath, Shemoth: the fortieth degree; verse fifteen.

15. You must **anoint** them, just as you anointed their father (all priests and kings as well, were Anointed Ones or Christs, if you will…), so that they may serve me as priests: for their anointing will certainly be a perpetual priesthood.

Of all we've read thus far, we have yet to read anything about mothers, daughters, sisters, or wives, for with the exception of prophetess, a woman can only serve in one or more of any of these four positions, but not as a priestess; for there were never any priestesses in ancient Yishrayil.

Now for **Tribal Lineage** we will read the book of Numbers: the thirty-sixth degree in its entirety:

1. The chief fathers of the families of the children of Gilead, the son of Makhir, the son of Manasseh, of the families of the sons of Yahsiph, Joseph, came near, and spoke before Mosheh, and before the princes, the chief fathers of the children of Yishrayil:

2. And they said, Yah commanded *Mosheh* to give the land for an inheritance by lot to the children of Yishrayil: and *Mosheh* was commanded by Yah to give the inheritance of Tzalaphakhad, Zelophehad our brother to his daughters.

3. And if they be married to any of the sons of the other tribes of the children of Yishrayil, then will their inheritance be taken from the inheritance of our fathers, and will be put to the inheritance of the tribe whereto they are received: so will it be taken from the lot of our inheritance.

4. And when **the jubilee of the children of Yishrayil** will be, then will their inheritance be put to the inheritance of the tribe whereto they are received: so will their inheritance be taken away from the inheritance of the tribe of our fathers.

5. And Mosheh commanded the children of Yishrayil according to the word of Yah, saying, the tribe of the sons of Yahsiph have spoken well.

6. This is the thing which Yah commands concerning the daughters of Zelophehad, saying, "Let them marry to whom they think best; only to the family of the tribe of their father will they marry."

7. This way the inheritance of the children of Yishrayil will not be removed from tribe to tribe: every one of the children of Yishrayil will keep himself to the inheritance of the tribe of his fathers.

8. And every daughter, that possesses an inheritance in any tribe of the children of Yishrayil, will be wife to one of the family of the tribe of her father, that the children of Yishrayil may enjoy every man the inheritance of his fathers.

9. Neither will the inheritance remove from one tribe to another tribe; but everyone of the tribes of the children of Yishrayil will keep himself to his own inheritance.

10. Even as Yah commanded Mosheh, so did the daughters of Zelophehad:

11. For Mahlah, Tirtsah, Khaglah, Malikah, and Nuwah, the daughters of Zelophehad, were married to their father's brothers' sons:

12. And they were married into the families of the sons of Manasseh the son of Yahsiph, and their inheritance remained in the tribe of the family of their father.

13. These are the commandments and the judgments, which Yah commanded by the hand of Mosheh to the children of Yishrayil in the plains of Maab by Yardan near Yariykhah.

The fact that the daughters of Tzalaphakhad, Zelophehad inherited their father's property doesn't prove that genealogy can be passed through daughters; in fact to the contrary, this is clarified in the book of Numbers: the thirty-sixth degree, verses six to eight; where they are specifically instructed to marry someone from their father's tribe or their inheritance would pass from theirs to another. With such we are left with not even one scriptural reference tracing tribal lineage through women, and this because, according to The Law of Yahuwah [Gen.2:18, 3:16], it is a woman's duty to be an assistant to her husband.

This point is further bolstered in the book of Bamidbar, Numbers: the first degree; the eighteenth verse, where we're shown how the Yishrayilites declared their pedigrees according to their father's houses.

And they assembled the entire congregation on the first day of the second month, and they declared their pedigrees after their families, by the house of their fathers, according to the number of the names, from twenty years old and upward, by their polls.

And now for **Royal Lineage**:

Genesis, Barashiyth: the forty-ninth degree; verse eight to twelve.

10. The scepter will not depart from Yahuwdah, nor will a lawgiver from between his feet, until Shiloh (he to whom tribute is due) come; and to him will be the gathering of the people (By means of scripture study [Jeremiah and 2nd Kings], the royal scepter remained with the tribe of Yahuwdah, until the eleventh year of the reign of Malik Tzidqiyahuw, Zadakiyah, Zedekiah, who was the last Anointed-one/Messiah of Yishrayil. He reigned just before the carrying away into Babylon, approximately 586 BCE; and this is "the gathering of the people", that was spoken of in this prophecy. Unfortunate for the children of Yishrayil, but by the righteous will of Yahuwah, authority was given to Nebuchadnezzar, the Anointed-one/Messiah of Babylon; meaning he was the one to whom tribute, at that time was due; again fulfilling the prophecy of the patriarch, and having nothing to do with Jesus Christ, nor anyone else named to such authority).

The First Book of The Chronicles: the seventeenth chapter; verses eleven to nineteen.

11. What will occur when your days have expired is that you will go to be with your fathers, and I will establish your seed after you – it will be one of your sons; and I will establish his kingdom.
12. He will build a house for Me (only one son of Dawiyd built a house for The Name of Yah), and I will establish his throne forever.
13. I will be his Father, and he will be My son: and I will not take My mercy away from him, as I took it from him that was before you (Malik Shawl, Shaul, Saul was king before Dawiyd):
14. I will set him over My House and in My Kingdom forever: and his throne will be established for evermore.
15. According to all these words, and according to all this vision, so did Nathan speak to Dawiyd.
16. And Dawiyd the king came and sat before Yah, and said, "Who am I, O Mighty One, and what is my house, that You have brought me here?

17. And yet this was a small thing in Your eyes, O Mighty One; for You have also spoken of Your servant's house for a great while to come, and have regarded me according to the estate of a man of high degree, O Father Yah.

18. What more can I (Dawiyd) say to You for the honor You have shown Your servant?

19. O Mighty One, for Your servant's sake, and according to Your own heart You have done all this greatness, in making known all these wonderful things.

The First Book of The Kings: the eleventh chapter; the forth verse.

4. When Shalomon was old his wives turned his heart after hinder gods; and his heart was not fully with Yah his Heavenly Father, as was the heart of his father Dawiyd.

A final point here is that when Queen Athalyah wanted to eliminate the Royal Line of Dawiyd, she only killed the males knowing full well that a female descendant of Dawiyd couldn't pass on the right to the throne. This was recorded in The Second Book of The Kings of Yishrayil; the eleventh chapter, and in The Second Book of Chronicles; the twenty-second chapter.

3) Though you may not have noticed it, the third problem has already presented itself where we examined the royal lineage of The Messiah; the fact that even if it could be maintained that a family line might be passed on through the mother, Mary herself was not from a legitimate messianic family. According to Scripture, The Messiah must be a descendant of King Dawiyd through his son Shaluwman, he was the one that built the temple, not Nathan.

We may see this explained in The Second Book of Samuel: the seventh chapter; verses twelve and thirteen.

12. When your life is over and you sleep with your fathers, I will raise up your offspring to succeed you; he will proceed from your own body, and I will establish his kingdom.

13. He will build a house for My Name (only one son of David ever built a house for Yah's Name), and I will establish the throne of his kingdom forever (Here we see one of the attributes our Uncle Nate had in common with Jesus, that is that neither of them ever had a throne established in Yishrayil).

In First Chronicles: the seventeenth chapter; verses eleven to fourteen.

11. And it will come to pass, when your life has expired and you have gone to be with your fathers that I will raise up your offspring to succeed you, which will be of your sons; and I will establish his kingdom.

12. He will build a house for me, and I will establish his throne forever.

13. I will be his Father, and he will be My Son: and I will not take My Mercy away from him, as I took it from him that was before you [Remember that Malik Dawiyd was not the first but the second king of Yishrayil; Shawl, Saul was first. Because Yah was displeased with Shaul He took the kingdom from him and gave it to Dawiyd. Christian ignorance or amnesia in this area leads them to believe that Tahallal, Psalm one-hundred ten; verse one is speaking of Jesus while quoting Yah's command to "Sit at My right hand" (the seat of the first-born son), but of course Dawiyd was speaking of Shaul not JC. Then Shalomon in First Kings: the fifth chapter; the third verse reveals that this exact sentiment was also spoken of his father Dawiyd, all the royal lineage of Yishrayil, and Yishrayil as a whole; Ex.4:22]:

14. But I will settle him in My House and in My Kingdom forever: and his throne will be established for evermore.

First Chronicles: the twenty-second chapter; verse ten.

10. He will build a house for My Name; and he will be My Son, and I will be his Father; and I will establish the throne of his kingdom over Yishrayil forever.

First Chronicles: the twenty-eighth chapter; verses four to seven.

 4. However Yah, Mighty-One of Yishrayil chose me over everyone in my father's house to be king over Yishrayil forever: because he has chosen Yahuwdah to be ruler; and of the house of Yahuwdah, the house of my father; and among the sons of my father it pleased Him to make me king over all Yishrayil:

5. And of all my sons – Yah has given me many sons; He has chosen Shalamah, Shilomoh, Shalomon my son to sit on the throne of The Kingdom of Yah over Yishrayil.

6. He said to me, "Shalomon, your son, will build My House and My Courts: for I have chosen him to be My Son, and I will be his Father."

7. Moreover I will establish his kingdom forever, **on condition** that he never ceases to keep My Laws and My Judgments, as at this day.

Oh my brothers and sisters, surely you too can now see the glaring evidence of the facts. That which is recorded in the book of Matthew – the genealogy of Joseph is traced back to King Dawiyd through his son Shalomon, but then down to the cursed King Jeconiah, and at the end of the day, Joe wasn't actually Jesus's father anyway. The most significant problem in Luke's version, if not already obvious, is that even if one wanted to maintain the belief that Luke is tracing the genealogy of Mary, and that it is possible to pass on genealogical lineage through the mother, Mary would still be of no assistance to Jesus, because her bloodline does not go back to David through Solomon. It also seems quite contrary, and downright negligent of the other New Testament writers, never to have even once mentioned the magnanimous advent of his immaculate conception.

According to "The Word" of Yah and that of all His prophets, the principle notion of "Jesus" has failed to fulfill any of the four major messianic prophecies:

1) With the exception of locution, he was never *"anointed"* as Priest, High-Priest, Prophet or King; he never ruled Yishrayil. Even he is alleged to have confessed (John. 18:36), "My kingdom is not of this world". If this is so, why should it concern us who are equally as "of this world" as were Abraham,

Yitzkhaq, and Yishrayil? These men also looked forward to an earthly inheritance and kingdom of Yah. Which of the prophets of Yah encouraged any expectation of a "Kingdom Come" to any place other than this world? None of the prophets of Yah spoke or wrote of human inheritance of any extraterrestrial kingdom; in other words, you never hear of a, "Kingdom of Heaven", until you fool around over there in that "New Test".

2) He never established "**Peace on Earth**" as Yishayahuw, Isaiah prophesied in the eleventh chapter: verses six to nine.

3) He was never preceded by the return of the prophet Aaliyahuw, Elijah, as Malakiyahuw, Malakyah, Malachi said he would be in the fourth chapter; the fifth verse.

4) I will send you Aaliyahuw, Elijah the prophet before the coming of the great and dreadful day of Yah:

5) And finally, he has been disqualified from ever being a messianic candidate due to his lack of necessary genetic background.

Now with the acquisition of knowledge, we are confronted with "Freedom of Choice": Either we may continue to accept that "The Word of Yah" is correct when it promised the children of Yishrayil a messiah from the House of Dawiyd through his son Shalomon, or we may choose to "**believe**" that Yah has for some mysterious reason changed (Mal.3:6) and will not honor "The Word".

While some may believe our objective here is to dampen their faith, I can assure you that this is far from the truth; instead it is to encourage "The Very Elect" to continue the honest, open-minded and willing search for the deeper truths cleverly disguised in these allegories. I also hope to illustrate the fact that not all questions can be answered with short snippets and sound bites, as many, in this age of instant gratification have grown accustomed, but instead require protracted, composed and gradual explanations. For example: If you take the few moments necessary to contrast and compare the genealogical lists of Matt vs Luke, which I have for your convenience, printed and placed below in columns. One can barely help but notice the various and glaring discrepancies and inconsistencies found therein.

Matthew 1: 1-16	Luke 3:23-31
Dawiyd	*Dawiyd*
Shalomon	**Nathan**
Roboam	Mattatha
Abia	Menan
Asa	Melea
Josaphat	**Eliakim**
Joram	Jonan
Ozias	Joseph
Joatham	Juda
Achaz	Simeon
Ezekias	Levi
Manasses	Matthat
Amon	Jorim
Josias	Eliezer
Jecohnias	Jose
Salathiel	Er
Zorobabel	Elmodam
Abiud Cosam	Addi
Eliakim	Melchi
Azor	Neri
Sadoc	**Salathiel**
Achim	**Zorobabel**
Eliud	Rhesa
Eleazar	Joanna
Matthan	Juda
Yaaqob	Joseph
Joseph	Semei
Jesus	Mattathias
	Maath
	Nagge
	Esli
	Naum
	Amos
	Mattathias
	Joseph
	Janna
	Melchi
	Levi
	Matthat
	Heli
	Joseph
	Jesus

At the conclusion of this study, I was left with seven additional questions that I'd like to share with you:

1) Why is it that, while Matthew was able to bring forth his baby Jesus in twenty-eight generations (7×4=28), Luke needed forty-three (7×6+1=43, Jesus being "The One" over the multiple of seven. With the generational ratio of 28:43, and a guesstimation of 30 yrs per generation, that's an approximate 450 year difference in time)?

2) Why did Matthew say that Joseph's father's name was Yaaqob, but Luke says his name was, Heli?

3) Though Matthew and Luke agree that Zorobabel was Salathiel's son, Matthew says Jecohniah was the father of Salathiel, yet Luke says that Salathiel's father's name was Neri?

4) Tahallal, Psalm one-hundred ten; verse four speaks of The Order of Malakzadak, Melchizedek, which is not merely an individual, as many have been misled by "false prophets" and the King James version to "**believe**", but is actually an Order of priests, a member of which had made acquaintance with one Ibrahiym Bin Tharakh/Azar, and whose ministry is associated with an enigmatic temple known as HYKL AL ILYWN, Hayakal Al Ilyuwn, Temple of The Most High. Of this temple is found no census or earthly ancestral records, for which cause, and rightfully so, it is postulated that this order, having extraterrestrial origins is positioned so that we have no way of knowing their population count, nor may we be certain of their lineage. If indeed Jesus is of this "Order", whose peaceful kingdom is not of this world, why then would Matthew and Luke spend so much time and effort, the greater part of two chapters respectively, elaborating on an earthly genealogy?

5) How is it possible for any researcher worthy of the title to compile a genealogical list of descent from David to Jesus and never once mention Solomon, under whose governance The Temple of Yahuwah was built?

6) Deuteronomy: the seventeenth degree; verse fifteen says,

15. Be sure to set a king over you whom Yahuwah your Mighty-One chooses. He must be from among your own brothers. He must not be a foreigner (a god, ghost or an angel) who is not your brother.

Deuteronomy: the eighteenth degree; verses fifteen to eighteen says,

18. I (Yah) will raise up a Prophet from among their brothers, **like you** (Mosheh), and will put My words in his mouth; and he will speak to them all that **I** (Yah) will command him.

But if you have read this research paper along with your Bible, you have seen with your own eyes, and have reasoned with your own mind, how difficult; in fact it is impossible to prove that the genealogies depicted by Matthew and Luke may be used to show authentic blood relations between Jesus and the children of either Yishrayil, or any other terrestrial nation. "The New Testament" claim that his father was either an angel, ghost or god indicates that not only was his father not from among the children of Yishrayil, but that he wasn't even human; which is yet another disqualifier.

This point is further embellished by the phrase found in verse eighteen above, "like you"; but discrepancies between the two, Mashah, Mosheh, Moses and Yahawashi, Yahuwashi, Yahuwshuah, Yahoshuah, Yahshuah, Yeshuah, Joshua, Yesus, Jesus, Isa can in many places throughout the Bible, easily be found and illustrated. The first of many is the fact that, Mosheh's Levitical genealogy is well documented in the Torah; in Shemoth, Exodus: the sixth degree; verses twenty to twenty-seven, and Jesus's genealogy is not only questionable but impossible. As we've already seen, when we read the genealogy of JC, we find that not only was he not from among any of the tribes of the nation of Yishrayil, but according to the story, DNA evidence would prove he was of an extraterrestrial species; not even human. Mosheh taught only what Yah told him to, yet Jesus frequently used terms like, "verily **I** say unto you", thereby teaching his own doctrine and frequently exalting himself not only to the level of Yah, but on numerous occasions blatantly usurping authority over not only Mosheh, and the prophets, but over Yah Himself; and if one were to echo the notion of he and Yah being one and the same, then among other things, we'd have to question the address of his prayers [To whom did Jesus pray, and to whom did he teach his students to pray? Was it not, "Our Father, which art in heaven?"].

An example of blatant attempts to usurp authority over Mosheh and Yah is recorded in Matthew 5: 21-37:

21. You have heard that it was said by **them of old time**, you must not kill; and whosoever kills will be in danger of the judgment:

22. **But I say** to you, that whosoever is angry with his brother without a cause will be in danger of the judgment: and whosoever will say to his brother, Raca ["F" (forget) you], will be in danger of the council: but whosoever will say, you fool, will be in danger of hell fire.

23. Therefore if you bring your gift to the altar, and there remember that your brother has anything against you;

24. Leave your gift there before the altar, and go your way; first be reconciled to your brother, and then come and offer your gift.

25. Agree with your adversary quickly, whiles you are there with him; in case your adversary deliver you to the judge, and the judge deliver you to the officer, and you be cast into prison.

26. Truly I say to you, you will never come out there until you have paid your last penny.

27. You have heard that it was said by **them of old time**, you must not commit adultery:

28. **But I say** to you, whosoever looks at a woman with lust has committed adultery with her already in his mind.

29. So if your right eye causes you to offend, gouge it out, and throw it from you: for it is better for you that one of your members perish, than for your whole body to be cast into the grave.

30. Or if you right hand offends you, cut it off, and throw it from you: for it is better for you that one of your members perishes, than for your whole body to be cast into the grave.

31. It has been said, "Whosoever will divorce his wife, he must give her a certificate of divorce":

32. **But I say** to you, "Whosoever divorces his wife, unless it is for the cause of fornication, causes her to commit adultery: and whosoever will marry her that is divorced commits adultery.

33. Again, you have heard that it has been said by **them of old time**, "You must not forswear yourself, but must perform your oaths to Yah":

34. **But I say**, "Do not bind yourself with any oath at all; not by heaven; for it is Yah's throne:

35. Nor by the earth; for it is his footstool: neither by Jerusalem; for it is the city of the great King.

36. Neither bind an oath by your head, because you cannot make one hair white or black.

37. But let your "yes" mean "yes" and your "no" mean "no": for anything more than this becomes evil.

While some may argue that there was a reasonably valid point or two made in the verses above, we also see a couple of fundamentally questionable and redundant phrases; 1) "them of old time". Who was he referring to when he said, "them of old time"? The answer is Yahuwah, Mosheh and all The Prophets of Yah. So we see that JC is clearly alleged to have been speaking against Yahuwah and Mosheh, and then proceeds to assert his own ideas over both Yahuwah and Mosheh, when he says, 2) "But I say..."

But I say? Like that song from the nineteen-seventies, "Jesus Christ, Superstar, who in the world do you think you are?" Surely this is the character of one who imagines himself to have usurped authority over Yah and His servants; the prophets.

The list of distinct differences between Mosheh and Jesus goes on much further than I care to write-out here and now, however I'm sure with the level of intelligence that I know you possess, you see my point; the conclusion of which, is that the verses referenced above from Deuteronomy: seventeen and eighteen also require clarification as to being intentionally vague, non-specific, generalized, hypothetical descriptions of any and all potential priests, prophets and/or messiahs, passed, present, and future; having absolutely nothing specifically to do with the Christ of the Roman/Greek writings, so called "New Testament".

In no way intending to be unduly harsh, I must confess being here reminiscent of yet another portion of the book of Matthew that has also proven problematic to say the least; that is the sixteenth chapter: verses twenty-seven & twenty-eight. Now for those who may not be familiar with this portion, Jesus is here depicted as being in the midst of a lecture to a captive audience when he says:

27. The Son of man (implicitly speaking of himself in the third person) will come in the glory of his Father with his angels; and then he will reward every man according to his works [Will Jesus punish the orthodox for worshiping Yah alone? To whom did King David and Solomon pray? Did they pray in Jesus's name, or will their ignorance be excused?].
28. Emphatically I say to you, there are some standing here, who will not experience death before witnessing the Son of man
coming in his kingdom.

So now as we approach the mark of two thousand years since this lecture is alleged to have occurred, every member of said audience having long since transpired, and after many others, whom I'll here call "false prophets", for having so often made false reference to just such an "end time". Every so often we've heard these self-proclaimed prophets and prognosticators predict the end of the world, and this having yet to be seen, forces us to ask, "Where is this kingdom, and where is its Anointed One?" The answer that I will soon make clear is encoded in one of the scriptural references that we've already covered earlier in this study; Yishayahuw, Isaiah: the eleventh chapter: verses one to nine, but this time with strictest focus starting at verse six.

6. The wolf also will dwell with the lamb, and the leopard will lie down with the kid; and the calf and the young lion and the fatling together; and a little child will lead them.
7. The cow and the bear will feed; their young ones will lie down together: and the lion will eat straw like the ox.
8. The nursing child will play near the hole of an asp, and the weaned child will put his hand on the viper's den.

9. They will not hurt nor destroy anything in my entire holy mountain: for the earth will be as full of the knowledge of Yah, as the waters that cover the sea.

Being an avid nature lover, having been introduced by my father, and thus having been a frequent viewer of nature documentaries since my early childhood, I have yet to see any wild carnivore harmoniously dwelling with any herbivore, accept that is, with the expedient intent of ingestion. Is it fair that in order for the lion to live, the gazelle must die? I don't know whether or not it is fair. I do know that it is life. Therefore the more significant question is, which of the two positions is more preferable? Would you rather be the lion, or the gazelle? Contrary to those who have convinced themselves and others to "**believe**" that the earth is yet approaching six thousand years of age, carnivores have consumed herbivores for millions of years. In any case, even if I am wrong concerning this chronology, it is undoubtedly true at the present time, and will certainly remain this way throughout the foreseeable future.

Again, the question is: When will Jesus return? The answer is: When wolves dwell peacefully with lambs, and when leopards lie down with kids. When a calf, young lion and fatling play together, and a little child leads them. When a cow and a bear chew cud together; while watching their young ones rest (Bears are omnivorous, and having but one stomach, it is impossible to chew cud. This is as opposed to the bovine, that by means of the transference of previously chewed grain throughout their four stomachs, being respectively regurgitated; the ruminated substance is defined as cud, and is chewed routinely as part of their digestive system). When will Jesus return? When a rainbow burns the stars out of the sky. When a lion eats straw like an ox. When the ocean covers every mountain. When a nursing child plays near the hole of an asp, and a weaned child puts his hand in a viper's den without parental concern. When the sun rises in the west, and sets in the east. When the sea goes dry, and mountains blow in the wind like leaves. When dolphins fly through forests, and parrots dwell at sea. When a dream is life, and life is a dream. When Day is Night, and Night is Day. When there's no more violence on the earth, and the earth is as full of the knowledge of Yah, as the water that covers it. The earth's surface is 75% water, and when the earth is 75% full of the knowledge of Yah; in just such a time will your Jesus return, for it is impossible to return to a place one has never been. It is written in your own scripture and yet you doubt it.

In plain English: Just as energy can never be created nor dissipated, and it is instead transformed from state to state, so it is that the present empire will eventually transpire following those that came previously, but at no time is anyone named Jesus coming to save your donkey, mule, or ass, and if anyone comes presenting themselves in a way that convinces you of such, you will once again have successfully been bamboozled.

The conclusion of this portion of the study also includes yet a seventh question and that is as follows:

7) Could all the shifting sand found throughout the examination of these genealogies be the reason that in the writings supposedly attributed to one, Shaul of Tarshish; also known as Paul, whose word frequently seems to be exalted over that of Yah, Moses, and even The Christ of the New Testament; that's The First Letter of Shaul To Timothy: the first chapter; the fourth verse, and his letter to Titus: the third chapter; the ninth verse, the writers, editors, translators, and redactors of the Roman/Greek writing's so-called, "New Testament", in an attempt to have all their bases covered, discourage us from asking questions and putting forth any effort into the study of the above given genealogies?

The reason for this type of genealogical discouragement is the same as it has been since the beginning of ourstory; they who govern this world don't want us to have the level of consciousness wherein like gods, we can think (Gen.3:22). They don't want us to benefit from the nourishment gained by the consumption of the fruit of the knowledge of a dualistic universe, in-which forces that seem to oppose one another, actually support and uphold one another; righteousness and wickedness being but one example wherein one cannot exist without the other. If it were left up to the Elohiym, we would have remained on an animalistic level of consciousness and wouldn't even know the difference between clothing and nakedness. Our mortality; the short lived; strict limitation of our time on this currently experienced plane of existence is significant, but if we had never acquired dualistic knowledge; knowing the difference between good and evil, or if we don't even know the difference between clothing and nakedness, then we would have never truly lived; at least not so on a godly level of consciousness (Ps.82:6). Christianity was forced upon us in order to keep us ignorant and enslaved. If one studies the history of Christianity, and many other world religions, it is plain to see that many initiates were converted by means of coercion of choice to either do so, pursue exile, or die. Our ancestors were neither Christian nor Muslim previous to this latest captivity, which is yet another detail in the explanation of our presence in this predicament. As a very brief paraphrased version of the invention of Christianity, I like to elaborate the story this way: In approximately 313 CE, the Roman Emperor Constantine decided to combine all the worlds religions as well as possible in order to form one "World Religion". The end result was then, and yet remains Christianity.

5. Paganism

Deuteronomy 12:1-32

"These are the statutes and rules that you must do in the land that Yahuwah, has given you to possess, all the days that you live on the earth. You must surely destroy all the places (of worship; church, mosque, temple, synagogue) where the nations whom you will dispossess served their gods, on the high mountains and on the hills and under every green tree (grove). You must tear down their altars and dash in pieces their pillars and burn their Asherim with fire. You must chop down the carved images of their gods and destroy their name out of that place. You must not worship Yahuwah in that way, but you must seek the place that Yahuwah will choose out of all your tribes to put his name and make his habitation there. There you must go…

Yeremyah, Jeremiah10:1-10

Hear the word which Yahuwah speaks to you, Oh house of Yishrayil. So says Yahuwah, Do not learn the way of the nations, and do not be amazed at the signs of the heavens; for the nations are amazed at them. The customs of those people are vain; for one cuts a tree out of the forest with an ax, the work of the hands of the workman. They adorn it with silver and with gold; they fasten it with nails and hammers, so that it will not wobble. They are like a rounded post, and they cannot speak. They must surely be lifted, because they cannot walk. Do not be afraid of them; for they can do neither evil or good, for it is not in them. There is none like You, Yahuwah; You are great, and Your name is great in might. Who would not fear You, O King of nations? For fear belongs to You, because among all the wise men of the nations, and in all their kingdoms, there is none like You. They are foolish and animalistic; the tree is an example of vanity. Silver beaten into plates is brought from

Tarshish, and gold from Uphaz, the work of the workman, and of the hands of the goldsmith. Blue and purple is their clothing; they are all the work of skillful ones, but Yahuwah is the true Power; He is **The Living Power, and Everlasting King**. At His wrath the earth will tremble, and the nations will not withstand His fury.

Instead you celebrate their Helladays, the worst of which being Christmas, Easter, and Halloween, at which celebrations you dress in costumes like the dead and dying, and/or you eat their detestable things, and now you find yourselves wondering why you're sick. Can you deny bowing down to the Christmas Tree? How do the gifts get there, or how are they removed less you bow down beneath the tree? The Corona Virus came through and shutdown all your places of worship; from mosque, to temple, church and synagogue, and all of you, having submitted to the deep state rulers of this world, may now speak only in hypocrisy concerning the power of your gods. They wouldn't even allow you to make the Hodge to Mecca, and yet you still can't see that Yah is not with you, and His blessings are not upon you. In such ways, the governments of the world demonstrate their lack of concern for your religion, and they display true authority as all were forced to "render unto Caesar". Like the musical artist Prince said, "Hurricane Annie ripped the ceiling off a church and killed everyone inside". This was his way of saying that these places; church, mosque, temple, synagogue, are but like any other building, and only in your imagination, are they holy. Even the Pope, who is the number one perpetrator of idolatry, remains shielded behind bullet proof glass when in public place; apparently the idols serve as no protection.

In approximately 313 CE, in order to quell, what was for all intents and purposes, a civil/religious war between monotheistic Christians, and polytheistic Pagans, the Roman Emperor Constantine, though he was born, raised, and maintained Pagan rituals and beliefs throughout his life, sought a pragmatic way to bring peace to Rome. By 325 CE the Ecumenical Council at Nicaea was assembled to combine the best of all the worlds religions, including Ancient Egyptian, Hebraism, and Paganism, in order to form a World Religion; the end result was then and remains Christianity. After Christianity was formed, the mission immediately became world-wide conversion. The goal was then and yet remains to convert every living human being to said religion. To their credit, the Romans did not discriminate on this goal. Toward this regard, one's previous identity was irrelevant, as was the nation one claimed as descent, along with the skin tone one possessed; the only criteria, by penalty of death, was the acceptance of the newly proclaimed edict; "Jesus Christ is The Son of God", and in his absence, "The Pope of Rome is The Vicar of Christ".

Whether we are under the influence of the denominations initiated by the Roman Emperor Constantine, and the Ecumenical Council at Nicaea in 313-325, or by those of the Protestant Baptists of John Smyth in 1608, the Mormons of Joseph Smith in 1830, the Seventh Day Adventists of William Miller in 1863, the Jehovah's Witnesses of Charles T Russel in 1872, or that of the Pentecostals of Charles Parham in 1901; all of the common era, all equally paganistic, and equally idolatrous. For those of us that identify as Hebrew Yishrayiliym, any person, place, or thing, if it is other than Yah and Yah alone, then it is an idol, and due to this fact, those in leadership positions in such organizations, as well as their followers are idolaters.

Each and every time the species known as Man has found himself in trouble, it was Yah and Yah alone that saved him. When Man found himself lonely, and unable to reproduce, it was Yah Who gave him a woman (Gen.2:22). When Man found himself naked, it was Yah Who clothed him (Gen.3:21). When Man was to be put to death for unauthorized acquisition of knowledge, it was Yah Who suspended the sentence, and eventually granted his pardoned (Gen.3:23). When the earth was to be inundated by a catastrophic flood, it was Yah Who gave him the forewarning, and the diagrams for his means of salvation (Gen.6:10-22). There's no way to count the number of times He saved Abraham, Yitzkhaq, Yishrayil, Mosheh, David, and the prophets, etc. Each and every time the children of Yishrayil repented of their sins, it was Yah Who freed them from their many captivities. It is Yah Who has mercifully preserved us alive as it is this day; even though we and our forefathers have continued to live in violation of the agreed upon "Blood Oath/Covenant"; also known as an "Unbreakable Vow", the penalty for which is death, and when Yah says, "enough", the time will come to free us again, hopefully for the last time, it will again be Yah alone. The bottom line is this; anyone or anything that you bow down to, worship, and serve, if it is not Yah, then that one, that group, or thing is an idol (Deut.28:64).

While watching the documentary of the Nuremberg Trial, I was disturbed by a strange and perhaps perverse form of jealousy for my people, and I realized that this must certainly be what Mosheh was translating when he wrote, Deuteronomy 32:21:

21. They have moved me to jealousy with worthless gods; they have provoked me to anger with their vanities, so I will move them to jealousy with an amalgamated people; I will provoke them to anger with a people that had been barbaric gentiles.

Nevertheless we must be grateful to Yahuwah for His utilization of the European converts to Judaism, for if not for the preservation of Yah's Law by means of their zealous observation of the same, then it is possible that we may have left ourselves totally deprived of any other reference point. For their efforts, as no good deed goes unpunished, they suffered the holocaust of the early nineteen forties, in which six million of them were systematically murdered by Nazi Germany and its collaborators.

Throughout this document, you've probably noticed that I've frequently underscored the word "believe". This is because I have so often been asked by Evangelistic Christians, Mormons, Jehovah's Witnesses, Seventh Day Adventists, etc., who all frequently tend to the question, "Do you 'believe' in Jesus Christ?" Whether the answer is "Yes" or "No", while I could always provide the diminutive answer they seek, I usually op to explain that, "When belief verses substantiation, I am partial to substantiation". You see, the origin of their question is from a view of life, which is an offshoot from the world of "Fantasy" and "Make Believe", where as if we were children, we are encouraged to "believe" in fables, fairy-tales, legends and myths like The Tooth Fairy, The Easter Bunny, the Boogeyman, and Treasures in Heaven. The myth of Santa Clause is so culturally interwoven, that parents insist on having their children write letters of solicitation, and even NORAD is said to be complicit in tracking the route of his world-wide deliveries to, "all the good little children". Truthfully, all this is done in order to compel those same parents to enrich the economy of the already wealthy merchants, who aided by this means, hope to empty their store shelves. At some point, most of us became disappointingly knowledgeable of the fact that, our elders had been misleading us; these weren't true stories as literally seen in reality.

Yeremyah, Jeremiah 16:19:

Oh Yahuwah, my strength, and my fortress, and my refuge in the day of affliction, the Gentiles (the so-called, "White People"), and those under their influence, will come to you from the ends of the earth, and will say, **Surely our fathers have inherited lies**, vanity, and things wherein there is no profit.

Some of us come to realize that, all of the above mentioned are but allegories and metaphors designed to explain the various cycles of the Sun, Moon, Stars and Earth, and the correspondence to which we ought to harmonize with them; "As above, so below", but these legends are created to do so in a way that teaches and/or renders comfort to inexperienced and/or willfully ignorant minds. Despite proof to the contrary, we may choose to believe anything, but substantiation of facts produces the potential of more intelligent responses to the realities of life, enabling us to acquire providence of actual solutions for the real problems we encounter. This is not to say that the allegorical lessons contained in myths and legends aren't worthy of consideration, but that when they are viewed as literal, factual and/or historical people, places and things, the deeper, esoteric and occult teachings back of them are too easily concealed from the audience. The ruling class has always been aware of the fact that, what the conscious mind believes, the subconscious mind acts on, therefore, if a person believes something that isn't true, their subconscious mind will compel them to act upon that misinformation.

For those who may be interested, here's what I believe: In order to support one another's beliefs, believers must gather in groups, while "knowers", those in possession of substantial knowledge are often forced to stand alone. I also believe that if we are honest with ourselves, and if we are open-minded enough to willingly sit down together at the table of reason, open our Bibles and other authoritative writings, and read them for what is actually written, as opposed to what we've previously been programmed to believe, then it will frequently be proven that we had previously been deceived by a government that determined to either enslave or kill us by any means necessary. The deceptions that have been revealed in this report are but the tip of an enormous iceberg that has been perpetuated throughout human existence. At the top of the social pyramid dwell the one percent of the population that controls ninety-nine percent of the world's resources, wealth, and power. They continue the same policies and programs in-which the vast majority are indoctrinated from the moment of birth. It is simply the deprogramming of innate truth, and reprogramming of damnable lies, and all in order to maintain the perpetual state of ignorance, scarcity, and slavery, opposed to knowledge, abundance, and freedom.

Their goal is to keep us deeply embedded, from cradle to grave if possible, in a world of ignorance, myth and fantasy. Using thoroughly established, tried and true diversionary scare tactics, like those used to corral herd animals, employed in religion and superstition; threats of social and religious anathema, brimstone, hellfire and so forth; in this way, our ignorance is weaponized against us. They cast stumbling blocks before the blind, while they continue to rape, rob and pillage each and every natural resource and mineral available; utilizing the same for themselves, their families and fraternal associations. I see this perpetuation of ignorance as the greatest of sins, and public revelation of such knowledge has brought about the demise and/or martyrdom of far too many of those who miraculously "woke" from the dream state, hoping to assist their neighbor in doing the same. Whistle Blowers like, Abraham Lincoln, Martin Luther King, Malik Shabazz, John Lennon, John and Robert Kennedy, The Musical Artists known as Prince, Kanye West, and Michael Jackson, Edward Snowden, Colin Kaepernick, Kyrie Irving, and Julian Assange are just a few nameable in modern times. Throughout ourstory, most of them died or had their lives ruined in recognition of the question, "What happens when the majority no longer fear the minority?"

Many other questions persist, but confidently trusting in your knowledge and ability, I leave it up to you to find both the questions and their answers; and according to the dictates of mercy, you will present them to me. However, though I remain confident that many messiahs, a term which simply means "anointed-one", are yet to come, and that many anointed-ones, Christs, if I may indulge in usage of such a term, have already come; every priest, prophet, and king of Yishrayil, was and is an Anointed-one, a Christ. In light of the information stated above concerning the cannibalism, human sacrifice, idolatry, messy genealogy, and paganism that is Religion, Christianity most specifically, since it is the most prevalent; if I will here forward utilize the term "Messianic", in reference to my chosen faith and life-style, it must not be seen as indicative of any belief on my part, that the factitious character of the Roman/Greek writings, whom we had previously been taught to call Jesus was/is he.

At this point, I want to thank everyone again for not merely walking the initial mile, but the extra mile through this study with me, and for those who might seek even further clarity and truth, for we must never accept the word of but one witness, I therefore encourage all to checkout the following website: www.covertmessiah.com. Another one of many great presentations is called "Caesar's Messiah" on YouTube. Also recommended on YouTube is Brother YHWHudah's dissertation on "The Jesus Myth", on his channel called YHWHOURRIGHTEOUSNESS. Ray Hagins is yet another one of many enlightened souls that have become aware of the existence and perpetuation of this modern mythology.

As always in closing I say,

Halleluyah! Halleluyah! Halleluyah!
Praise Yahuwah to whom praise is due, all praise
is due to Yahuwah!
Praise Yahuwah in the name of Yahuwah;
for there is no greater name in heaven,
or upon the earth by which man may be saved.

HALLELUYAH!